CHOOSING
TO LIVE THE
BLESSING

Co-author of the best-seller, The Blessing

JOHN Ph.D.
TRENT

*Bring the Gift of Light
and Life to Every Relationship*

CHOOSING
TO LIVE THE
BLESSING

141549

WATERBROOK
PRESS

Colorado Springs

CHOOSING TO LIVE THE BLESSING
PUBLISHED BY WATERBROOK PRESS
5446 North Academy Blvd., Suite 200
Colorado Springs, Colorado 80908
A division of Bantam Doubleday Dell Publishing Group, Inc.

To Doug Barram, who first showed me a picture of Christ's love.
To my precious wife, Cindy, who pictures every day what I prayed for
in a godly wife.
And in special memory of my mother, Zoa,
who filled my life with boxes full of loving snapshots.
I love you, Mom.

Contents

---

31 Days to Living the Blessing

Acknowledgments

IN THIS BOOK in particular, I would need many more pages than I'm allowed to list everyone I'm thankful for. But for starters, I couldn't have had a more supportive group behind me than my friends at WaterBrook Press. Dan Rich, Thomas Womack, Liz Heaney, Rebecca Price, Doug Gabbert, Ginia Hairston, Nancy Guthrie, and the rest of the team believed, prayed, and worked tirelessly to pull this book together. That's *while* they were building a wonderful publishing house from the ground up. I'm honored to be in your "first season" of books and to be a part of your team.

Here in Arizona, a special word of thanks for my long-suffering office manager, Marty Kertesz. She and our Encouraging Words board members and prayer team prayed and pulled for me throughout. Then there are faithful friends like Doug Childress, Mark Wheeler, Darrell Heringer, and Ron Gardner, as well as the men in our CrossTrainers Bible study who are always the first to be subjected to my rough drafts.

Ken Gire deserves his own page for his last minute heroics and help, as do my literary agents and friends, Greg Johnson and Rick Christian.

Finally, Kari and Laura deserve special mention for their patience with Dad as he finished this book. Your mom and I couldn't have two more wonderful daughters.

If it is true that photographic pictures have changed our lives, we wanted to know why. How have photographs shaped our personal histories and our collective imagination? How do we read pictures? What do we read from them?

Marvin Heiferman and Carol Kismaric

Talking Pictures: People Speak About the Photographs That Speak to Them

To Be a Person of Blessing

Almost twenty years ago I was an intern at a psychiatric hospital. There, daily doses of viewing broken dreams and shattered hearts were a part of each shift.

Then an incredible thing happened in my life.

I was getting ready to teach a Bible study at our home church. We were going through the book of Genesis, and I came upon chapter 27.

It was the story—actually an unforgettable picture—of two boys desperately struggling to get the same thing.

Their father's blessing.

Though I'd read the story of Jacob and Esau dozens of times, that day it was as if I were *standing* inside the tent.

I could see Esau's eyes light up when he heard at long last that it was time to receive his blessing.

I saw Rebecca gather her robes and run through the hot sand, grabbing Jacob, her favorite. Furiously they invented a plan to deceive his father.

I could smell the meal Jacob brought his father and stood amazed as the doubting Isaac finally set aside his questions ("Are you *really* my son Esau?") and gave Jacob a wonderful blessing.

Then I saw Jacob go out one side of the tent just as his brother rushed in from the other with his own savory offering for his father.

Esau's face was lit with expectation.

His smile nearly split his face as he asked for his blessing.

And I saw the look of shock, then disbelief, and finally rage wash over him as he realized he would never . . . *ever* . . . get his father's blessing.

I saw all this in that snapshot in the Scriptures because I'd *lived* it in so many ways over so many years.

Esau's heart-wrenching cry, *"Bless me, even me also, O my father!"* was what *I* had been crying out in my heart of hearts since I was a child.

The concept of the blessing suddenly blossomed before me.

There it was. A biblical way of looking at my life that answered so many of my inner struggles. Although unable to name it until then, I had sought my father's blessing a hundred times and more. I had longed for it. Lived for it for years. And yet always it remained just out of reach.

Then I realized that Esau's cry was not just an echo of my own heartache. It went to the heart of the life stories I was hearing each day in the psychiatric hospital. Men and women saying . . . *crying* . . . *begging* in their brokenness.

"Bless me, Mom. . . . Bless me, Dad. . . . *Please!*"

If you have read my previous books, you know that began my study of the blessing. I first looked at it as strictly a parenting tool. It became the subject of my doctoral dissertation and then the focus of the book *The Gift of the Blessing,* coauthored with my good friend Gary Smalley.

And the blessing is an incredibly powerful parenting tool.

However, after nearly two decades of teaching, studying, and praying through the blessing, I've come to see that it's not *just* a parenting tool, as important as that is.

It's a gift we're called to give *every* person. It's a lifestyle that Christ chose, one we're *called* to follow.

A CALLING AND A CHOICE

Our choosing to bless our children can create life-shaping experiences for them. *Choosing to live the blessing each day can be a life-changing experience for us.* And that's what you'll discover in this book. How to live out the blessing every day, in every relationship.

First, because it's our calling.

The apostle Peter, looking back at the unforgettable pictures he saw of Christ's suffering, wrote, "Do not repay evil with evil or insult with insult, but with blessing, because to this you were called so that you may inherit a blessing" (1 Peter 3:9, NIV).

To be a person of blessing is our calling.

Listen to the way Eugene Peterson in his eminently readable paraphrase, *The Message,* translates these same verses: "No retaliation. No sharp-tongued sarcasm. Instead, bless—that's your job, to bless. You'll be a blessing and also get a blessing."

Think about that for a moment.

"That's your job, to bless."

You may have sworn it was to be a heavy-equipment operator or homemaker or policewoman or physician or computer designer. But your job is actually to bless. It's your calling. And in doing so, you'll see the blessing come back from God himself.

But there's more.

It's also a choice, a choice set before us in every relationship—when we meet with our pastor or the postman, with our best friend or a casual acquaintance. It's a choice we make when people cut us off in traffic or come through when we need them most.

There is a dramatic picture in Scripture where Almighty God had the nation of Israel stand on two mountains, facing each other like opposing fans at the Super Bowl. Then he said, "I call heaven and earth to witness against you today, that I have set before you life and death, the blessing and the curse. So choose life. . . , you and your descendants" (Deuteronomy 30:19).

They couldn't miss the picture God gave them that day. As they stood within a mile of taking their first steps in the Promised Land, God illustrated that every step would involve a choice. A choice that would affect not only the quality of their lives and relationships but their ultimate ends. It was a choice to be obedient to his Word. To reflect his love and lifestyle and to pass that way of living down to their children. To stand distinct from all other nations and people.

It's a choice set before us as well.

The choices we make to bless or curse others are also being watched. Every day. By our coworkers. Our families. Even, as the Scriptures tell us, by a great cloud of witnesses.

PICTURES ARE A KEY TO OUR CHOICES

How, then, do we understand and live out this choice to bless others?

When it comes to the blessing, God provided pictures to help us understand his words and thoughts. The picture of Jacob and Esau wrestling over the same gift. The picture of thousands of people standing on opposite sides of a valley. As we'll see, the pictures of ungodliness that Josiah was given but refused to follow, and the priceless pictures we have of Christ blessing a hemorrhaging woman, a woman at a well, his disciples, and even the people who nailed him to the cross.

In our own lives the pictures we've collected affect everything from the professions we enter, to the people we marry, to the people we become.

Simply put, to bless others is to leave a picture full of light and life in their lives. For regardless of where we are, we're always leaving pictures in other people's lives. And they're always leaving them in ours.

Sometimes the pictures are as subtle as a glance. Other times they are as obvious as a billboard. But whether they are subtle or obvious, seen once or over a lifetime, in grainy black and white or in glowing Technicolor, pictures have a profound impact on us all.

So I've centered the book around this theme of pictures. Our ability to live out the blessing depends upon the choices we make about . . .

the pictures we are left with,

the pictures we are blessed with,

and the pictures we leave behind.

PICTURES THAT THE HEART REMEMBERS

Let me illustrate why pictures play such a powerful role in choosing to live our calling and how understanding them can greatly help our ability to bless others.

I think of a picture taken by an amateur photographer who worked in the loan department of a bank. Hearing an explosion at 9:02 in the morning, Chuck Porter instinctively grabbed his camera and rushed from his office.

From the streets he saw a freeze frame of stopped traffic. Shattered windows. Daggers of glass on the sidewalk. People spilling out of office buildings, terror in their eyes. And two-and-a-half blocks away, a cloud of dust eating block after block of downtown.

He sprinted to the scene of the explosion. And between 9:15 and 10, he chronicled with his camera the shock, the confusion, the horror. When he ran out of film, he hurried to a one-hour photo lab to have it processed. He fidgeted in the waiting area for the pictures to be developed. When the employees in the lab brought him the pictures, tears were streaming down their faces. The images were heartbreaking. Especially one of them.

The one of a fireman cradling a rag doll in his arms. Except it wasn't a doll. It was a baby. Somebody's love and dreams, somebody's joy and prayers. Somebody's baby. Lying there in the arms of a stranger. Limp and covered with blood.

Who can forget that picture that day at the scene of the Oklahoma City bombing?[1] That horrifying picture assaulted our senses from the cover of *Time*. Shocked us as we bought our coffee in convenience stores. Took our breath away as we stood in checkout lines at the grocery store.

That picture would go around the world, capturing in an image what a thousand words never could.

In that one picture we felt the tragedy. We felt something of the parents' horror . . . something of the city's violation . . . something of the community's devastation . . . something of the nation's shock and outrage.

The point is, we felt *something*. We *all* felt something.

Something saddening, something sickening, something beyond the power of words to express.

And we felt it because of a picture.

A picture has the power not only to convey more information than words but different information. Information that is not only emotional but often subliminal. Information that is stored within the caverns of our subconscious, seeping to the surface in all sorts of ways. Like the best of dreams . . . or the worst of nightmares.

If we were to sit at a well-worn kitchen table, a cup of coffee or hot chocolate in hand, and talk face to face, I'm sure we could each share pictures from our past.

Right now, think back on a picture that brought life and light into your life, a picture of blessing.

Perhaps your blessing picture is of being a kid on Christmas morning. The smell of pine filling the living room. The sound of a toy train chugging along the tracks around the tree. Sagging strings of lights winking with excitement.

Remember how you felt that morning when the present wasn't underwear or socks or something practical? When it was the BB gun you had circled in the Sears catalog? The one your parents said was out of the question?

Or when it was the doll that came with a wardrobe and clothes and furniture that you had wished for and prayed for but knew your parents couldn't afford so you never begged them? Brought it up but never begged.

Remember the feeling—that tingly, bubbly feeling you couldn't hide? You couldn't keep still, couldn't keep from running next door to share your excitement.

Pictures of blessing like that come back in full color, telling you that you were very valuable. Greatly loved. Deeply appreciated.

Pictures that back then and even today add weight and substance and a secure foundation for our deepest selves, affecting our view and treatment of others and the way we respond to God.

But we also carry other pictures. Pictures that tantalize us but don't come close to satisfying. Pictures that leave us feeling angry . . . betrayed . . . without hope. Pictures that leave us feeling cursed.

For example, perhaps your pictures of Christmas weren't of love and warmth.

Maybe you have a torn picture, where one of your parents wasn't there, didn't drop by, didn't call. Maybe you have pictures of a parent who was hung over, whose words slurred and breath stank. Maybe your holidays were filled with the tension of a failing marriage. Behind-closed-door arguments with an unfaithful spouse. Out-in-the-open arguments about "How are we going to pay for all this?" Parents fighting, children crying.

The heart remembers those words, those pictures, those moments of humiliation, as well as the moments of celebration. The heart is like that cardboard box in the closet where we keep the photographs we've taken but haven't had time to sort through and organize.

Day after day, week after week, year after year, pictures are dropped into that box. Polaroids. Olan Mills specials. Rolls of Instamatics. Pictures of birthdays. Christmas mornings. The first Little League game. The first and only piano recital. The last-day-of-school party. The most exhilarating moment. The most embarrassing one. The overexposed. The underexposed. The ones with the wrong film speed. Ones when the flash didn't go off. The faded. The blurred. The stories of our lives. At least in part.

By the time we reach adulthood, the box is bulging with memories. We take those memories with us everywhere we go. Memories of a parent's smile . . . or scowl. Memories of a teacher's praise . . . or ridicule. Memories of a classmate's kindness . . . or cruelty.

Pictures that carry a blessing or convey a curse.

We take those emotionally charged pictures to every stocking we fill at Christmas, to every plate we empty at Thanksgiving. We take them on every job interview, on every date, on every vacation. To every reunion. Every discussion. Every argument.

Everywhere we go, they go with us. And we never know when one of those pictures may come back to haunt and hold us back . . . or bring us happiness.

Pictures—the beautiful sunlit ones and the dark horrible ones and all the shades in between—affect the way we think, the way we feel, and the way we perceive the world, other people, and most importantly ourselves.

That is the power of a picture.

The power to bless or to curse.

And that is why if we're to live out the blessing—to make it our everyday job—our hearts need to remember the pictures we were left with. That's our first step.

MY OWN HEART REMEMBERS

This book includes my best recollection of pictures from my family album. Maybe my mind hasn't captured the exact way things happened. Maybe the pictures I took between the ages of six and seventeen weren't shot with a steady hand or from the right angle or in the proper lighting. Maybe the years between then and now have had an effect too. Who knows? But this is how I remember them.

I hope you enjoy looking at these pictures from my own and others' albums—pictures that I pray will teach, encourage, and inspire. And I pray that this most personal of all my books blesses you in a most personal way.

PART 1

The Pictures We're Left With

THERE'S AN OLD SAYING: "Water can't rise above its source."

Think about that for a moment. As a law of nature, it's a simple reality. But when it's applied to people's lives, it becomes a terrible truth. People do struggle to rise above what they've been given.

If we've never seen how to love, it can be extremely difficult to express loving actions or thoughts. If we've been told all our lives we're worthless, untalented, or ugly, carrying the weight of those words can seem like lugging gallons of water. Weighing us down. Washing away our confidence. Flooding our deepest selves with discouragement and hopelessness.

If we're truly to become people who bless others every day, we must understand the sources that have shaped our lives. Did we receive love and affirmation and encouragement? The kind of support that filled our hearts and acted like the locks in a river? Locks that stop the downhill flow and raise the water level higher and higher until even mighty ships are lifted up and carried inland?

Do you feel like your life has been filled to overflowing, lifting you up, carrying you forward into the future with confidence? Or do the pictures in your past drain you of energy and leave you stuck and floundering in the sticky mud of criticism or neglect?

In this section I want you to look at the pictures you have been given. To go back to your source and see clearly the memories and moments that have shaped where you've been . . . and perhaps who you've become. For so strong and so shaping can these early pictures be that to talk about blessing others in the present often becomes a wish not a reality. We may want to bless someone with a positive future, but we'll fail if we don't believe we have a special future ourselves. So our blessing to others becomes paper thin and tears into pieces when we try to hand it off to another.

Above all, I want you to see in my error-filled life (as well as in some pictures from Scripture) that water *can* rise above its source. The love of God, expressed in his only Son, can lift up your head, pull you out of the mud, and wash away feelings of shame and hopelessness.

Because of him, you can become a person who blesses others.

Even if you've never received the blessings yourself.

Memory is a central part of the brain's attempt to make sense of experience, and to tell coherent stories about it. These tales are all we have of our pasts, and so they are potent determinants of how we view ourselves and what we do. Yet our stories are built from different ingredients: snippets of what actually happened, thoughts about what might have happened, and beliefs that guide us as we attempt to remember. Our memories are fragile but powerful products of what we recall from the past, believe about the present, and imagine about the future.

Daniel L. Schacter

Searching for Memory

"It's Your Dad"

The movie *Field of Dreams* had a powerful effect on a lot of people. Myself included. The story is about a lot of things. Baseball. Nostalgia. America's past. But most of all it is about the healing of memories.

On one level it tells about the healing of a professional wound left behind when eight members of the White Sox were ejected from baseball for conspiring to throw the 1919 World Series. On another level it tells about the healing of a relational wound left behind when a father was taken out of his son's life by a fatal heart attack.

The mother had died when the boy was three, leaving his father to raise him. The son had some good memories of his father, like being put to bed with stories of Babe Ruth, Ty Cobb, and Shoeless Joe Jackson, being taken to baseball games, and playing catch. But as the boy grew up, other memories overshadowed those. Memories of disagreements and arguments and leaving home in rebellion.

The father died while the son was experiencing the '60s at Berkeley. Along with some deep-seated resentment, there was regret for the words that had been spoken. And for those that never were. What was left in the son's heart was an ache, a longing. One more chance for a game of catch. For a conversation. For a relationship.

The movie opens with a montage of memories—old photograph albums, home movies, single pictures that milestoned the past. The first picture in the album is a closeup of a boy in coveralls, a black-and-white photograph that has turned sepia with age. As the now-adult boy tells his story through pictures and voice-over narration, the camera pulls back to reveal the boy sitting cross-legged in a field.

The boy was born in 1952, the same year I was born.

The next picture, neatly matted, is of a soldier standing in a doorway somewhere in France during World War I. Standing young and lean. Sharply dressed in his military uniform. Looking every bit a hero—at least in the eyes of that cross-legged little boy.

When I was that boy's age, the fields I sat in, played in, dreamed in, were the slopes of Camelback Mountain in Phoenix, Arizona. It was there my brothers and I played army, challenging other neighborhoods to war. On that battlefield we built forts, planned ambushes, set booby traps. With dirt clods as hand grenades, along with our bazookas, machine guns, and a volley of sound effects, we fought the enemy.

Our dream of being heroes was lived out on those fields.

It was a great place to grow up. Neighborhoods were safe, playmates were plentiful, and summer days stretched forever. What a great time to be a kid.

The kid I once was, who grew up there, grew up never knowing his father. He left when I was two months old. Left a wife and three young boys. He left her to bathe us, feed us, clothe us. Left her to nurse us when we were sick, tutor us when we couldn't understand our homework, discipline us when we got out of line. Left her to provide for us, protect us, point us in the right direction.

If anyone was ever equal to such a task, it was my mom. Her name was Zoa. It means life. She gave it to each of us. And so much more than mere biological life.

I never heard her speak negatively about my dad. But she never spoke openly about him either. If his name came up in conversation, she said only that Mom and Dad didn't live together anymore. She never said why. And she never assessed blame.

I don't remember missing my father, at least in those early years. How can you miss something you've never had, someone you've never known? I grew up not knowing what he looked like or sounded like, how tall he was or what color hair he had. There were no pictures of him in the house. Not on the walls. Not on the bookshelves. Not even in the scrapbooks.

THE ONE PICTURE OF MY DAD

One day while rummaging through the house for a game, I opened one of my mother's drawers. In the drawer was a sheaf of papers, and it was their oldness, I think, that intrigued me. The yellowing newsprint. The mustiness of another era. The crumbling mystery of it all. As a boy with a rich fantasy life, I was certain I had stumbled upon something important. Treasure maps, maybe. Coded messages. Who knows what secrets were hidden there?

Leafing through the pages of my mother's past, I found a picture that had been scissored out of an Anderson, Indiana, newspaper. The man in the picture was a soldier, dressed in combat fatigues, and a captain or general or someone important was pinning a medal on him in the field.

Maybe it was because it was 1958 and pictures of soldiers still lived on the battlefields of our black-and-white television. Maybe it was because I was a boy who loved storming the hills of Camelback Mountain. Or maybe it was something deep inside, an inarticulate ache for something I had never had. I don't know. But the picture mesmerized me. I took it to my mom.

"Who's this?"

She took the picture in her hand, pausing a moment. She looked at me, returned the picture, then, as if she had known this moment would one day come, said, "It's your dad."

She told me the picture had been taken after the battle of Guadalcanal and that he was receiving a field decoration for bravery. The eighteen-year-old infantryman had risked his life to save a fellow soldier who had been wounded and pinned down by enemy fire. Dodging a hail of bullets, he picked up the soldier, threw him over his shoulder, and carried him to safety.

My hands trembled. They were touching the picture of a hero. A war hero. The very thought thrilled me. That this hero was my dad thrilled me even more. A newspaper had written up his story, taken his picture, spread the news to every doorstep of Anderson, Indiana. My dad was a decorated soldier who had stormed the beaches of Guadalcanal, dodging enemy fire. He had fought his way through the battlefield to reach a wounded buddy. And I knew that someday he would fight his way back and reach me. No matter what minefields he had to cross. No matter how many bullets he had to dodge.

That picture of him was the only one I had ever seen. And although my hands returned it, my heart held on to it. Every now and then I crept back to my mother's room, to that drawer, those papers, just to make sure the picture was still there and to kindle the hope that someday he would step out of that picture and into my life.

I held on to that hope through the end of elementary school. Through the end of junior high. And throughout high school. By that time my brothers and I were up to our shoulder pads in sports. Football, baseball, wrestling. I weighed only 140 pounds, but I made the all-city team as a linebacker, the all-district team as a wrestler, and started as catcher on the baseball team with my twin brother, Jeff, who was the pitcher. I was small, but I was a fighter. Just like my dad.

While Mom went to our practices, washed grass stains out of our uniforms, and cheered in the stands, I waited for Dad to fight his way home. Every game I waited. Every sport. Every father-son banquet. By now I not only missed my father, I was embarrassed at not having one. Embarrassed when fathers came down from the stands at the end of each game, looking for their sons to congratulate them or console them. Seeing them put their arms around their sons, patting them on the shoulder pads, walking them off the field. It was all so embarrassing. And painful. Knowing they were taking them to the drive-in for a burger. And afterward, taking them home.

How I longed for that, ached for that, waited for that.

Finally one fall day in my junior year, the waiting ended.

THE LONG-AWAITED CALL

"Zoa, this is Joe." The phone call came out of the blue, without warning, without explanation, without an apology for all the years he hadn't called, hadn't come by, hadn't communicated. "I live over by the stadium where the boys are playing, and I'd sure like to come and meet them. Would that be all right?"

A few days earlier the local newspaper had run an article about our upcoming game, and a reporter had come to our practice, bringing a photographer with him, who took a picture that ended up on the front page of the sports' section.

Jeff and John Trent—Twin Starters for the Mighty Titans.

The picture is what prompted the phone call. He said he wanted to watch my brother and me play, then we would all meet on the field afterward. After my father's call Mom spoke with the head coach and received permission for us to stay after the game instead of having to travel across town on the team bus.

The night before the game I hardly slept. He had played a year of college football before he went to the war, we learned. Now he was coming to watch us play. The day of the game I thought about little else. We played Westfield High that night. Danny White, who went on to become an All-American at Arizona State and from there to quarterback the Dallas Cowboys, led their team in a game that seesawed back and forth for three quarters. But in the final quarter Danny's soon-to-be legendary arm threw two touchdown passes. We went down in defeat. But we went down fighting.

Neither Jeff nor I was discouraged about the loss. We played our hearts out. Not for us, not for our team, our coach, our school. We played our hearts out for our dad. We wanted him to see the sons he hadn't seen for all these years and, when he saw them, to be proud.

After the game my mother and older brother came down from the stands to meet us. Together we walked to the place Dad had said he would meet us. It was a moment we had waited for all of our lives. We took off our helmets, hoping he would see us and somehow recognize us. While the fans streamed from the stands and onto the field, we searched for the hero who had finally fought his way home. As the streams thinned, our anticipation swelled.

I felt a mingling of anticipation and awkwardness, similar to what the grown-up son felt in the final scene of *Field of Dreams,* where he saw his father after so many years of separation. Remember the mingling of emotions?

"Look at him," Ray Kinsella says to his wife. "He's got his whole life in front of him, and I'm not even a glint in his eye. What do I say to him?"

What *do* you say at a moment like that? To a father you have never seen, never met, never talked to? Do you run to him, walk to him, wait for him to walk to you? Do you shake hands or hug, laugh or cry, talk about the game or the war? What?

While I was wondering such things, the bus left, and the parking lot emptied. The bleachers were bare now, row after row of them staring down at us, blankly, mockingly. Still we waited. Finally someone shut off the stadium lights, leaving the four of us standing on the field. On that dark, empty field.

He didn't show.

He was my father and a hero . . . and he didn't show.

It is all backwards when a torn pattern—a spoiled pattern—is followed and handed down year after year, and people forget what the original pattern was like. It is all backwards when men turn from God because they can't stand the word father and thus attribute wrong things to God.

Edith Schaeffer, "What Is a Father?"

A Way of Seeing

THREE

Out of Control

That night when the lights went out on the football field, the lights went out on my dreams. Until then I never blamed my father for leaving us, never was angry at him or bitter or even hurt. But then, then it became a whole new ball game. He told us he would be there. He got our hopes up. Got us thinking that maybe we mattered, maybe he cared. And then he didn't even show.

Although my father had abandoned me—abandoned all of us—seventeen years before, I had never felt the pain of the abandonment. Now I did.

The ride home was quiet. The four of us were each dealing with our feelings in our own way. Which was a quiet way. As close as Jeff and I were, we didn't talk about that night, how we felt, how we hurt. Years later when we were in college, we did. But not that night. And not any night of the two remaining years we spent at home.

By the time we drove home, I could have ripped the front door off its hinges. *How could he? How could he leave us there, standing by ourselves, making fools of ourselves?*

Everyone on the team knew why we weren't going back on the bus that night. The coach knew, the players, the managers—everyone. What was I going to tell them Monday morning when they asked how it went with my dad, what was it like seeing him after all those years, and was he coming home, moving in?

I cursed his name and cursed God for passing it on to me. Son of a Trent. *You can have your name. Go ahead, take it. You've taken everything else.* I called him every rotten name I knew, and I knew plenty. All that night I wrestled with the bedsheets. I could have punched him; I was that mad. But I only had a pillow.

STRUGGLING TO SURVIVE

The family my father had left behind struggled to be a family the best we could, struggled to make ends meet, to work things out, to take whatever life sent our way and make the best of it. We struggled, in a word, to survive. Our way of surviving was not to talk about the negatives, only the positives. What we didn't talk about among ourselves we were left to ourselves to figure out. Which is the way a lot of families survive. It was the way Frederick Buechner's family survived the suicide of his father. In his autobiographical book, *Telling Secrets,* Buechner tells the story.

> There was no funeral to mark his death and put a period at the end
> of the sentence that had been his life, and as far as I can remember,
> once he had died my mother, brother, and I rarely talked about him
> much ever again, either to each other or to anybody else. It made my
> mother too sad to talk about him, and since there was already more
> than enough sadness to go round, my brother and I avoided the
> subject with her as she avoided it for her own reasons with us. . . .
> We didn't talk about my father with each other, and we didn't
> talk about him outside the family either partly at least because
> suicide was looked on as something a little shabby and shameful in
> those days. Nice people weren't supposed to get mixed up with it. . . .
> His suicide was a secret we nonetheless tried to keep the best we
> could, and after a while my father himself became such a secret. . . .
> Within a year of his death I seem to have forgotten what he
> looked like except for certain photographs of him, to have
> forgotten what his voice sounded like and what it had been like to
> be with him. Because none of the three of us ever talked about how

we felt about him when he was alive or how we felt about him now that he wasn't, those feelings soon disappeared too and went underground with the memories.[1]

The memory of that dark Friday night on that empty football field went underground too. But it didn't stay there. Neither did the feelings.

The feelings I had before that night were mostly positive. Mom had given us a lot of love, a lot of memories. Good memories. Some of my fondest were the times Mom would take us to the library, where she looked for books to help her with the battles she was forced to fight. The battle of a woman in the '50s and '60s, fighting for a career. The battle of a single parent rearing a houseful of boys. And the battle against rheumatoid arthritis, which was crippling her.

While she looked for her books, she let us roam the library, looking for ours. Where I looked most often was the section on World War II. Unconsciously I was building a bridge to the past, hoping I might meet my father somewhere back there. Maybe in a picture of Guadalcanal. Maybe in a story. I wanted so much to connect with him, and the library seemed the only place that even dimly remembered where he might be.

One of the other subliminal influences my father's war picture had on me was that I wanted to wear a uniform like he wore. But a boy can play soldiers only so long. After that, what battles does a growing boy fight, what uniforms does he wear?

A football uniform was the one I wore, and a hundred yards of stadium grass was my battlefield. Though my father wasn't at the games where I played or at the banquets where I was applauded, I always felt the press clippings and awards would one day make him proud of me. Maybe it was another bridge I was trying to build. And maybe those were the only materials I had to build it.

All I know is, when he didn't show, the bridge collapsed.

ACTIVITY BECAME MY DRUG OF CHOICE

The hurt I felt that night turned almost instantaneously to anger, which I bottled as bitterness. I was like a shaken soda bottle, waiting for someone, daring someone to pry off the cap. When that happened, everything bottled up inside spewed out. Where it happened most often was the football field.

I threw myself into each football game with reckless abandon. One game in particular comes to mind.

On the opening kickoff, I sprinted downfield, my eyes searching for the ball carrier with almost predatory intensity. When a guy on the other team caught the ball, my eyes locked on him, and my feet instinctively tracked him. I chased him down, then dove at him full speed from his blind side. I struck him the split second he planted his leg, hitting him so hard his leg snapped. I ran to our sidelines, jumping in the air, while he lay where I left him, writhing on the ground. I felt the rush of the hunt and the thrill of first blood, but I felt nothing for him. Nothing of his pain. And nothing of the pain of his parents who had witnessed it so helplessly, so horrifically, from the stands.

Activity was the drug I used to deaden my feelings. I kept on the run, never allowing myself time to think about anything, to feel anything. I revved up the rpms on our '64 green VW bug and kept them revved until I coasted into the driveway late at night and fell into bed, exhausted. The amphetamine of activity that masked my pain also masked the pain in other people. I had no awareness of those around me, no understanding for them, no compassion, certainly no love or forgiveness.

I can see that now, looking back, especially when I look back on my relationships with girls. They were all short-lived, because as soon as the girl started getting serious, I dropped her. Except I would never tell her I had dropped her. Instead of meeting her after class to walk her to the next one, I just didn't show. I took another stairway, went down another hallway, simply avoided her. Never said a word. Never sent a note. Never made a phone call. In a few days, she got the message. It was all so easy. I simply walked another way to class. That way I didn't have to process anything, say anything, feel anything.

While I was so smoothly sidestepping the deeper issues in my life, my mom was having trouble just walking. The pain of her arthritis had grown debilitating, and she desperately needed surgery. Her uncle was a surgeon in Indiana, and since the surgery was expensive and the therapy extensive, she moved there for the remainder of the year. Her Aunt Dovey moved in.

For six months she looked after us, or tried to. And for six months I took it upon myself to be the one to ruffle Aunt Dovey's feathers. I treated her like dirt. I sneaked out almost every night, telling her off whenever she confronted me.

By now I was fluent in cursing and pretty good at telling people off. Today it may not seem like such a big deal for a teenager to curse, but back then if a coach heard you so much as whisper a swear word, you took a lap for it. Besides taking more laps that year, I lapped up more beer, getting drunk at parties and getting into trouble afterward. I got involved in stealing. Not because I wanted things, not material things anyway. I stole because I wanted something else. Acceptance maybe. Or maybe a family. Maybe that's why being in a gang appealed to me.

They called themselves "The Leaches," and to get in I had to steal a dozen gearshift knobs. Done. What next? Stereo? No sweat. The stereo we took was from an abandoned house, so we didn't think it a big deal. The police thought differently. Aunt Dovey tried to talk with me and help me the best she could, but I just stared a hole through her, spitting in defiance at the ground where she stood.

My callousness turned to harshness. At school one day I beat up a kid just for looking at me. After school I was worse, especially when I was with my drinking buddies. One night seven of us beat the Moody Blues out of a carload of longhairs from another school, smashed their car windows, and sped off laughing. I was so drunk I didn't remember much about it. The longhairs, however, did. When the police investigated the incident, they pulled me out of class for questioning. I didn't confess to what I had done, didn't rat on my friends. And I didn't feel anything for the guys I had whipped. But for the first time in a long time I felt something. It wasn't guilt, wasn't shame, wasn't remorse. It was embarrassment.

My life was out of control.

Aunt Dovey knew it.

I knew it.

Now the whole school knew it.

The word father should bring thoughts of one who is full of marvelous plans for the joy of his children—little joys day by day: the lunch together, the walk in the woods together, the game together, the book enjoyed together, as well as plans for longer periods of special fulfillment ahead.

Edith Schaeffer, "What Is a Father?"

A Way of Seeing

Jesus All Along

T he picture I was left with on the football field was more painful than all the ones without my father for the last seventeen years. For me it was a picture of a curse, one I tried to tear up and throw out. But no matter how I tried, I couldn't get rid of it. It lived in me, seethed in me. I was angry, so very, very angry.

"Anger," said Gerald Sittser in his book *A Grace Disguised,* "is simply another way of deflecting the pain, holding it off, fighting back at it. But the pain of loss is unrelenting. It stalks and chases until it catches us. It is as persistent as wind on the prairies, as constant as cold in the Antarctic, as erosive as a spring flood."[1]

The pain of losing my father was compounded by the fact that I was so close to getting him back. So close to filling in all those missing years, all those missing memories, all those Christmases and birthdays and ball games. When he didn't show up that night, the pain was so unrelenting I ran from it. But the pain stalked me. No matter how fast I ran or how far, it always caught up with me. When it did, the only thing I had to defend myself against it was anger. So I held my anger close. And although it was sheathed at my side, my hand was always on its hilt, ready to strike. I held on to that anger throughout my junior year.

Until Doug Barram disarmed me.

A PICTURE OF ANOTHER DAD

His stature alone was disarming. He stood six feet four inches tall and weighed probably 225. Right out of college, he was still in great shape from the years he had played offensive tackle. Doug was the Young Life leader at our high school. He was also the warmest, gentlest, most loving man I had ever met. He had an ever-present smile, bright eyes that were always glad to see me, a genuine enthusiasm in his voice, and huge arms that smothered me when he hugged me.

I first met Doug when I was a freshman. He would show up after school to watch the freshman football squad practice. A few members of the players' immediate families came to the games, but hardly anyone came to the practices. Doug was one of the conspicuous few. He stood on the sidelines, watching us, encouraging us, patting us on the shoulder pads and small-talking his way into our lives.

One picture particularly stands out in my memories of him. We had just lost a real heartbreaker of a game. I kept my helmet on because I was crying and didn't want anybody to see. Then running onto the field, this bear of a man came up to me, tears streaming down his face, and hugged me. It was Doug. I'd never seen a grown man cry before, let alone an athlete.

I saw Doug on the sidelines of my life a lot over my high school years. I still remember the delight in his eyes whenever he'd see me on the field, in the gym, at school. I still remember the excitement in his voice whenever he talked with me on the sidelines before the game or on the field after it. And not just me. I saw Doug befriend all sorts of people, people I wouldn't have wasted my breath saying "hi" to in the halls. But he said "hi." And he had the same excitement in his voice when he said it to them as when he said it to me, the same delight in his eyes, the same kindness, the same interest, the same genuineness.

From my freshman year through my sophomore year and into my junior year, Doug Barram left a lot of pictures in my life. He spent time with a number of us at the high school, talking about things that were important to *us*, laughing at things *we* thought were funny. He gave an open invitation for any of us who wanted a place to hang, to hang at his house.

For hours in his front yard we'd play "bull moose" football, a slow-motion game of tackle. Then we'd sit down and read the Bible, each with our own copy of a J. B. Phillips version, one we could understand, one we could underline, one he had given us.

He was the first man to give me a Bible. The first man to sit down and read it with me. The first man to ask me what *I* thought it said. The first man to pray with me. The first to show me what it meant to be a servant, a friend, a husband, a father, a man.

I saw him kiss his wife, tell her he loved her. And I knew it was true. I saw it in his eyes and saw it reflected in hers. I heard it in the tone of his voice as he said everything from "pass the butter" to "tell me about your day."

At dinner his whole family held hands and prayed, each person saying a sentence or two. The first time I ate at his dinner table was also the first time I ever prayed in a group. I stumbled over my words, getting out a few *pleases* and *thank yous* and *bless everyones*. My words sounded so hollow, so artificial, next to his. I knew his words were real because his pictures were real. Pictures of him standing on the sidelines. Pictures of him bundling up his kids at night, kissing them, wrestling with them, answering their questions, telling them stories, praying with them. I knew he meant every word, every hug, every prayer.

I knew whatever he had was real. And I knew it was something I wanted. I wanted so much to be around a man like that, a husband like that, a father like that. I wanted to be around it so much that every week or so I would drive to his house and mow his yard, just for an excuse to be there, just to see it all, just to experience what they had.

A family with a father. A father who showed up. A father who was there and who *loved* being there.

The pictures he left were so compelling. I only mowed his yard, but I would have painted his house, shingled his roof, cleaned out his garage, anything, anything just to be there and be a part of it, even if the part was just as a yard boy looking in from the outside.

THE PICTURE I SAW WAS JESUS

During my junior year when all that anger was working itself through my life, Doug invited my brother Jeff and me, along with a few other football players, to a religious film. Only we didn't know it was a religious film. He didn't tell us *that*. The film was terrible, the worst I had ever seen, or so I thought at the time. And by the time it was over, I was antsy to get out of there. But when the houselights came on, revealing a man standing in front of the theater, my heart sank. I knew I wouldn't be getting out of there anytime soon. The man gave a short testimonial, then gave us the opportunity to come forward and place our faith in Christ.

I thought as I sat there, *I still have my senior year ahead of me. The parties. The good times. The cruisin' and boozin'.* Nope. Wouldn't be me breaking ranks. I wedged myself a little more snugly into my velvet-cushioned seat. And from that seat I looked down the row at my brother Jeff. Then at my friends. Finally at Doug.

Then suddenly, unexpectedly, something moved me. I stood up. Jeff stood up. One of our friends stood up too. Filing out of our row and into the aisle, the three of us went forward. Doug trailed behind us, and when we reached the front of the theater, he talked with us and prayed with us, as one by one we gave our lives to Christ.

Something moved me that night at the theater. What was it? What was it that touched my heart and turned my life around? It wasn't the film. It wasn't the appeal of the man in the front of the theater. What then?

I think it was the cumulative effect of all the pictures Doug Barram had been leaving in my life. Pictures that said you matter, you have a place in my heart and at my table, what you think is important, why you hurt is important, who you are is important, to me, to my family, and to God.

In an instant the Holy Spirit brought those pictures together to form a composite. When I leaned forward and looked at Doug, the picture I saw was

Jesus. It was Jesus I had heard in Doug's voice. Jesus I had seen in his smile. Jesus I had felt in his hugs, in his home, in his heart. All along it was Jesus he was showing me.

I just never recognized him in a six-foot-four-inch frame.

I didn't know a lot about this Jesus. But I knew if I was ever going to have a home like Doug's, a marriage like his, a family like his, a life like his, I had to have in my heart what he had in his. I had to have Jesus.

No, it wasn't the film that moved me that night.

It wasn't the man in the front of the theater.

It was that composite of all the pictures Doug Barram had left in my life. That night they moved me. Out of my seat. Onto my knees. And into the kingdom of God.

We have no control over the stories into which we are born and little over those in which we are raised. They are as much an inheritance as our genetic code, creating roles for us to play as surely as our DNA maps a future for our bodies. . . .

We can change our stories only by changing our choices.

Daniel Taylor

The Healing Power of Stories

Choosing to Change

I wasn't sure what all happened that weekend at the movie theater. I wasn't sure how real it was or if it was real, what difference it would make in my life and if it did make a difference, how long it would last. I wasn't sure about any of those things.

Until the following Monday.

I was in P. E. class, playing tennis with this small, dorky guy who was beating the socks off me. Normally I would have done something like yell or curse, throw my racket into the net, grit my teeth, and give him a stare to melt a glacier. But I didn't do any of those things. By the middle of the game a sudden awareness swept over me. I wasn't angry. Not at him. Not at myself. Not at my racket. Not at anything. I couldn't believe it. I was getting beat . . . and I wasn't getting angry.

Only the week before I had been thrown out of a football game for my anger. I could never predict when it would erupt, much less control its eruption. My anger always seemed to be running just beneath the surface, like magma beneath the earth's crust, coursing to find an opening so it could vent itself. And it didn't need much of an opening. A sarcastic remark on the football field. A smirk in the hall. A lopsided score on the tennis court. But all of a sudden, there I was on the tennis court, on the lop side of the score, a small dorky guy on the other side of the net, acing me . . . and I wasn't angry. It gave me chills just thinking about it.

It also gave me the assurance that what had happened to me in that movie theater was real. That Jesus was real. That his love, his acceptance, his forgiveness, his power to change lives . . . all of it was real.

If anybody needed it to be real, I was the one. I'm convinced that the peer group of character qualities I was hanging with—the anger, the inability to forgive, the harshness and callousness—would have one day turned into a dangerous gang, leading me down some pretty dark alleys. Drugs maybe. Or some other form of addiction. Maybe even manslaughter. Prison. Who knows?

What I do know is this: "From within, out of the heart of men, proceed the evil thoughts, fornications, thefts, murders, adulteries, deeds of coveting and wickedness, as well as deceit, sensuality, envy, slander, pride and foolishness" (Mark 7:21-22). And before that night at the movie, the view from within was pretty scary.

Shortly before that night my dad finally did show up. He called to apologize about missing the game and asked for another time to get together. He picked a neutral site, a Chinese restaurant. It was a safe place to meet, safe from anybody's emotions spewing out, safe from confrontation, safe from the possibilities of the evening running long. I'll spare the details, saying only this. The best parts of the evening were awkward. The worst were embarrassing. And by the time we got to our fortune cookies, I had lost my appetite for the relationship that all my life I had hungered so much to have.

He had remarried, we were told. Had two kids, we were told. And for the past seventeen years he had lived within twenty miles of where we lived. Twenty miles from where we lived out our childhood. Twenty miles from where we played soldiers on Camelback Mountain, living on the hand-me-down hope that the hero would one day come home.

Twenty miles. And never a visit, never a call, never a card. Nothing.

Later we tried to get him to take a step or two back into our lives, but his steps were halting and didn't cover much distance. He invited us to his house, where we met his wife and kids. He and I didn't have a lot of common ground, except his involvement in the war and my interest in it. So that's what we talked about that night. Vietnam was raging on the other side of the world, on college campuses across the nation, and on the nightly news at home. As a kid who had grown up watching John Wayne fight his way through the Pacific, and who had stormed my own way over hill and dale of Camelback Mountain, the idea of going off to war seemed romantic. Maybe after my senior year I would even enlist.

WOULD MY FATHER'S STORY BECOME MINE?

The stories my dad told that evening were intoxicating. How they used to catch fish by throwing percussion grenades into the water. How when the grenade went off, the fish floated belly-up to the surface. How they cooked them in banana leaves. Stories like that.

But then the stories turned sober. He told about being under mortar attack and taking a direct hit to his foxhole that tore off his backpack and shredded his clothes. He barely escaped with his life. He told about replacements coming from the ship and how if they snored for two nights in a row they were "put on point," sent to lookout posts on the perimeter. Many of them never came back. You see, snoring lets the enemy know where you're hiding.

"You don't snore, do you?" he asked.

I said no, but the truth is, I didn't know. What if I did? And what if I got drafted? What if I snored two nights in a row and got "put on point"? Suddenly the reality of war fell into my thoughts like a mortar, shredding all my romantic notions.

The stories continued into the evening. Stories of how the Japanese would booby-trap jewelry boxes, map cases, anything that might appeal to an American soldier enough that he would pick it up for a closer look. He told about a time when he was out on patrol and some of his buddies came across a trove of trinkets. Before my dad could get there to stop them, the booby trap went off, killing two and mangling the rest.

Then he told of a time he was on his way to officer training camp. He was on a troop train, and many of the men had gotten drunk, celebrating their promotion from infantrymen to officer in training. When the train pulled into the depot, the commander was so infuriated he sent the train to boot camp. Everyone on that train went back as privates, back to the front lines, and back into combat. Three-fourths of them were killed.

I wondered as I listened. Would these be the stories I would be telling years from now? And would I someday become the man who was telling them now?

He was my biological father. I had always assumed I would become like him. He had given me life and half my genetic code. The code had determined my height and the color of my hair. What other things had it determined? Had it determined what kind of man I would become, what kind of father? Or did I have some say in the matter, some control over the story?

In his book *The Healing Power of Stories,* Daniel Taylor addresses those questions.

> Stories link past, present, and future in a way that tells us where we have been (even before we were born), where we are, and where we could be going.
>
> Our stories teach us that there is a place for us, that we fit. They suggest to us that our lives can have a plot. Stories turn mere chronology, one thing after another, into the purposeful action of plot, and thereby into meaning.
>
> If we discern a plot to our lives, we are more likely to take ourselves and our lives seriously. If nothing is connected, then nothing matters. Stories are the single best way humans have for accounting for our experience. They help us see how choices and events are tied together, why things are and how things could be.
>
> Healthy stories challenge us to be active characters, not passive victims or observers. Both the present and the future are determined by choices, and choice is the essence of character. If we see ourselves as active characters in our own stories, we can exercise our human freedom to choose a present and future for ourselves and for those we love that gives life meaning.[1]

Somewhere in my subconscious mind I looked at the pictures mounted on the page of the scrapbook that chronicled my junior year. I looked at Doug. I looked at my dad. They were such opposite pictures. They told such different stories. I didn't realize all of the implications of the choice I had made that night in the movie theater, but one of the implications was clear. When I got out of my seat and went forward, I made a choice about which picture I was going to live by.

I made a choice to change the story.

The moment the young child becomes reflective, however, is the moment the child begins developing the ability to choose rather than simply inherit a story. At the heart of reflection is the weighing of multiple possibilities— possible explanations, possible choices, possible consequences. The first suspicion that something could be different than it is signals the initial stirrings of character and the potential to choose one's story.

Daniel Taylor

The Healing Power of Stories

Switching Fathers

The choice I made at seventeen was similar to the choice Josiah made about the pictures in his life.

Except Josiah was eight.

Josiah was one of the rulers of the southern kingdom during the divided monarchy in Israel's history. The reign passed from father to son, generation after generation. Josiah had received it from his father, Amon, who had received it from his father, Manasseh. In 2 Kings 21, the Scriptures describe the reign of Josiah's grandfather.

Manasseh was twelve years old when he became king, and he reigned fifty-five years in Jerusalem; and his mother's name was Hephzibah. And he did evil in the sight of the LORD, according to the abominations of the nations whom the LORD dispossessed before the sons of Israel. For he rebuilt the high places which Hezekiah his father had destroyed; and he erected altars for Baal[1] and made an Asherah,[2] as Ahab king of Israel had done, and worshiped all the host of heaven and served them. And he built altars in the house of the LORD, of which the LORD had said, "In Jerusalem I will put My name." For he built altars for all the host of heaven in the two courts of the house of the LORD. And he made his son pass through the fire, practiced witchcraft and used divination, and dealt with mediums and spiritists. He did much evil in the sight of the LORD provoking Him to anger. (vv. 1-6)

Manasseh's reign was characterized by widespread apostasy and wholesale wickedness, with prostitutes offering their services in the temple and with children being offered as sacrifices just outside the city in the Valley of Hinnom. So great was the influence of Manasseh's wickedness that he caused the nation to do more evil than that done by the Canaanites whom God had driven out of the land centuries earlier (v. 9).

When Manasseh died, he was succeeded by his son Amon.

Amon was twenty-two years old when he became king, and he reigned two years in Jerusalem; and his mother's name was Meshullemeth the daughter of Haruz of Jotbah. And he did evil in the sight of the LORD, as Manasseh his father had done. For he walked in all the way that his father had walked, and served the idols that his father had served and worshiped them. So he forsook the LORD, the God of his fathers, and did not walk in the way of the LORD. (vv. 19-22)

A palace conspiracy cut short Amon's reign, and once again a young king ascended the throne. The account is recorded in 2 Kings 22.

Josiah was eight years old when he became king, and he reigned thirty-one years in Jerusalem; and his mother's name was Jedidah the daughter of Adaiah of Bozkath. And he did right in the sight of the LORD and walked in all the way of his father David, nor did he turn aside to the right or to the left. (vv. 1-2)

Did you notice what happened?

Josiah did not walk in the way of his grandfather, Manasseh, or in the way of his father, Amon. He walked in the way of *his father David*.

Josiah switched fathers.

A CHOICE TO LEAVE PICTURES OF BLESSING

When his father was murdered, Josiah inherited not only the throne but also a dark and distorted picture of what the person who sat on that throne should look like. But Josiah had a choice: He could live by the picture he was left with, or he could look through the family album for some other picture to live by.

To do so he needed to go back only a few generations, stopping at the picture of David, Israel's greatest king. David was a very human king. His life was filled with turmoil and tragedy, and he failed in many ways. But he always owned up to his failures and always humbled himself and sought forgiveness. He was a man with feet of clay, but at his very core he was a man after God's own heart (Acts 13:22).

Looking at the pictures, Josiah decided to step away from his physical father and into line with an ancestor with a decidedly spiritual lineage. In doing so, he changed the story of his life. When he made that choice, it enabled him to reverse the curse that had been handed him and to live out the blessing provided him through his forefather David. That choice not only changed his future, it changed the future of Israel.

> The three decades of Josiah's reign were among the happiest in
> Judah's experience. They were characterized by peace, prosperity, and
> reform. No outside enemies made war, the people could concentrate
> on constructive activity, and Josiah himself sought to please God by
> reinstituting matters commanded in the Mosaic Law.[3]

The choice Josiah made can't be mandated by committee, whether that committee is the Supreme Court or the local church. It's an individual choice. A choice to change the story by changing the pictures that influence the story.

What is so remarkable about the power of that choice is that it not only stops the flow of negative pictures handed down from one generation to the next, it *reverses* the flow. Not only can we can choose which pictures we live by, we can choose which pictures we leave behind.

The way Josiah did.

A record of some of those pictures is found in 2 Kings 23. So remarkable was his influence that the Scriptures memorialized him with this tribute: "And before him there was no king like him who turned to the LORD with all his heart and with all his soul and with all his might, according to the law of Moses; nor did any like him arise after him" (v. 25).

Not a bad caption for the pictures he left behind.

I'd settle for it in a heartbeat.

Thankfully, according to God's Word, we all can.

In another dramatic Old Testament story, God shared an amazing truth with his people. A truth Josiah would have read about in his public reading of the law.

Under the inspired leadership of Moses, the nation of Israel emerged from hundreds of years of slavery and crossed an inhospitable desert. But even then, their misery was compounded. For along the way, they received neither food nor water from the hands of those already living in the land. And one king in particular even hired a noted sorcerer, Balaam, to curse them.

But listen to God's words to his own in response to what they suffered: "The LORD your God would not listen to Balaam but turned the curse into a blessing for you, because the LORD your God loves you" (Deuteronomy 23:5, NIV).

His love reverses the curse.

It allows us to choose other pictures and pass them on as well.

Just like Josiah.

Horrible experience creates permanent mental pictures. . . .

The memory of trauma is shot with higher intensity light than is ordinary memory. And the film doesn't seem to disintegrate with the usual half-life of ordinary film. Only the best lenses are used, lenses that will pick up every last detail, every line, every wrinkle, and every fleck. There is more detail picked up during traumatic events than one would expect from the naked eye under ordinary circumstances.

Lenore Terr

Too Scared to Cry

Responding to the Pain

Compared to the life stories I've listened to in counseling, the pictures from my childhood weren't horrible. For that I am truly grateful. Some were difficult to bear, but none were unbearable. None were like the ones Henry Orenstein had to bear. In his book *I Shall Live,* he recalls his imprisonment and torture in a Nazi concentration camp. In the preface of the book he remarks:

> I wrote this book primarily from my own experiences, which for the most part are etched in my memory with unusual clarity. Some of the people and events from more than forty years ago are more vivid to me today than those of only yesterday. . . .
>
> A few events were so terrible and were buried so deep in my memory that only when someone who had shared the experience reminded me of them would the whole scene suddenly flash before me, intact in every detail and as fresh as though it were happening at that moment.[1]

Such is the incendiary power of the pictures stored in our memory, the power to flare up out of the smoldering ashes of our past. What do you do with such spontaneously combustible pictures? Do you leave them there, buried and smoldering? Or do you stir the embers and risk being engulfed in their flames?

The pictures of my father during the first seventeen years of my life were almost nonexistent. There was a certain pain associated with that, but the pain wasn't acute. It was more like a dull, chronic ache. Others, like Henry Orenstein, have survived pain that is so much worse. Concentration camps. Rape. The murder of a loved one. Years of battering from an alcoholic mate. Verbal and emotional abuse from a parent. Sexual abuse from someone they trusted. Terrible things, all of them. You don't have to have experienced the Holocaust to know suffering. You don't have to spend time in a concentration camp to know the shame, isolation, and torture of being in prison. They are different prisons, but they're still confining. Different suffering, but still painful.

For some, the pain is so unbearable they'll do anything to numb it. They'll fill every moment with work, every weekend with activity, anything to keep the past from having space to surface. They'll fill their bodies with drugs or alcohol or food. Or maybe deprive their bodies of food. Or go from one sexual distraction to another. On one level it's a "natural" choice to try to do anything that will immediately stop or hold back the pain. But we triple our pain by choosing sin over genuine (if more difficult) solutions. We can never run away from the pictures nor smear their image so much that they can't haunt us anymore.

Denial is a form of anesthesia. Sometimes denial is cloaked in self-confident assertions like "I've gone forward with my life" or "I've put the past behind me." But the problem with the past is that it never stays there. It has ways—sometimes subtle, sometimes intrusive—of resurfacing and wreaking havoc on the present. That is why some people seem stuck in a cycle of picking the wrong relationships, making the same mistakes, repeating the same patterns of self-destructive behavior. What they are really stuck in is the past. And they can't go forward until they go back there and begin dealing with some of those painful pictures.

"EVEN IN AUSCHWITZ WE HAD CHOICES"

For thirty years Edith Eva Eger tried to keep from going back there.[2] For thirty years she kept silent, holding those painful pictures inside her like a shameful secret. And for a lot of good reasons. She didn't want her children exposed to the horror she had experienced, didn't want them to feel different in school, didn't want them to be ashamed of their Jewish heritage.

On May 22, 1944, sixteen-year-old Edith Eva Eger, along with her mother and sister, entered the gates of Auschwitz in a cattle car packed with other Jews. As they were ordered from the railroad car, Josef Mengele motioned Edith's mother to the left line and Edith and her sister to the right. Edith instinctively followed her mother. Mengele stopped her. "Your mother is going to take a shower," he told her, turning her back to the other line.

Sometime later Edith asked a woman guard when she would see her mother again. The guard pointed to one of the gas chambers where smoke was curling into the air. "She's burning there now. Now you can talk about your mother in the past tense."

That moment was forever etched in young Edith's memory. That night it was followed by another one she would never forget. Learning that Edith was a ballerina, Mengele summoned her to perform for him. As she danced, she pretended she was at the Budapest Opera. It was her dream one day to perform there, and maybe dreaming she was there in her native land of Hungary was the only way she could have gotten through the evening. When she finished, Mengele dismissed her with a small piece of bread. Bread from the hand of the man responsible for killing her mother just hours before.

Edith spent nearly a year at Auschwitz and other camps before she was liberated. But deep down inside, where those memories were hidden, she was still a prisoner of her past. It was not until she finally looked back that she began to grieve.

"I grieve over the childhood I never had," she said years later. "I grieve over the fact that I danced for Dr. Mengele. I grieve that I was beaten so severely I couldn't dance anymore."

It was being asked to serve as a consultant on a stage play that made her look back. The play was about the Holocaust, but the focus of the play was on painful relationships. After seeing it performed in New York, she commented: "I feel it is important for everyone to see this play so they can go home and liberate themselves from their own concentration camps and to know they have choices. Many people today feel they have no choices. But even in Auschwitz we had choices."

Even in Auschwitz we had choices.

If they had choices in Auschwitz, then you and I also have choices even in the most abominable of conditions, even with the most abhorrent of memories.

In the cattle car on the way to Auschwitz, Edith's mother told her that no one could take from her what she put in her head. What you and I put in our heads is a choice. What will it be? Hatred or love? Bitterness or kindness? Vengeance or forgiveness? A curse or a blessing?

We can't control what happens to us, but we can control how we will respond to what happens. No one can take that away.

The choice is always ours.

When I saw this picture, it horrified me.

Dr. Benjamin Spock, about the photograph referred to in this chapter,

Talking Pictures: People Speak About the Photographs That Speak to Them

An Embrace Where Choices Meet

The photograph was taken in 1972, a year before the evacuation of American troops from Vietnam.[1] As I describe it, you will probably recall seeing it.

In the foreground, children are fleeing their village which has just been destroyed by napalm. The children are crying as they run. No, not crying. Wailing. American soldiers are walking behind them. And behind them, a spreading blackness rises from the charred remains of what was once the village of Trang Bang.

In the center of the photograph is a nine-year-old girl, her clothes burned from her body. Her arms are raw and welted from the napalm, and it looks as if the pain is so great she can't bring them to her side. *Terror* is the only word, if there is a word, that can describe the look on her face. She is running toward the camera, arms outstretched, naked and screaming.

It is a horrible picture. And when we first saw it, we were horrified. But other images flashed across our television screens, other magazine covers faced us at the checkout counters, other photographs filled the front pages. And we forgot the picture.

A Man Haunted by the Past

But not John Plummer. He couldn't forget. He was the man who had organized the raid that destroyed the village. He was the pilot of one of the helicopters responsible for the carnage, the burns, the screams.

Plummer thought the village had been cleared of civilians. The picture was proof it hadn't been. From the first time he saw the photograph, Plummer searched for that nine-year-old girl. For twenty-four years her picture haunted him, tormenting him with unspeakable shame, irrepressible guilt, and unrelenting nightmares. He turned to alcohol for relief, but the pain never left. Not for long anyway. Try as he could, he couldn't make peace with his past. He lost his self-respect. He lost his marriage. Maybe he would lose his mind.

To keep that from happening, he had to find peace. On Veteran's Day, 1996, he went to the Vietnam Veteran's Memorial to try to find it. While standing in the crowd, Plummer watched as one of the speakers stepped up to the microphone. And as she did, he trembled with emotion. It was the nine-year-old girl. She was thirty-three now and had come to lay a wreath at the memorial and to speak.

A Woman Who Chose to Forgive

Her name was Kim. Her full name, Phan Thi Kim Phuc. Kim told of the pain she had suffered and of the pain she suffers still. She told of others who had also suffered. Others in her village and surrounding areas. Others whose suffering was far more devastating than her own.

"Behind that picture of me," Kim told the crowd, "thousands and thousands of people . . . died. They lost parts of their bodies. Their whole lives were destroyed, and nobody took their picture."

Before she finished, she said she had forgiven the men who had bombed her village and covered her with burns. They were the words John Plummer had waited over two decades to hear. He plowed through the standing audience to reach her. When he finally did, they had only two minutes together before the police escort took Kim away.

In that brief encounter Kim saw the pain of John's past streaming down his face, and she reached out to hug him. All he could say was, "I'm sorry, I'm sorry, I'm sorry." And while he was saying that, she was saying, "It's all right; I forgive you."[2]

John and Kim started from opposite sides of the war to bridge the deep and terrible chasm that separates enemies. Each started with a choice. The one, to seek forgiveness. The other, to give it. Upon the bridge that both of them helped build, they met. And embraced. In that embrace they made peace not only with their past but with each other. The two exchanged addresses. They write each other, call each other, pray for each other. And to this day, they are good friends.

I can hardly imagine a more horrible picture to live with. But there are. There are people who live with the darkest and most devastating of memories. Memories of atrocities. Memories of abuse. Memories of abandonment. Each of them horrible in its own way. All of them haunting.

What do we do with pictures like that? What do we do with the pictures that leave us with a curse?

Where do we go to get the courage to look back on such a past?

Where do we get the strength to forgive?

Where?

A single picture has the power to stop us in our tracks and reveal to us just who we are.

Marvin Heiferman and Carole Kismaric

Talking Pictures: People Speak About the Photographs That Speak to Them

Healing for Going Forward

W hat do we do with a picture like the one John Plummer and Kim had to look back on?

Thumbing through the pages of the New Testament, we find that Jesus and Peter also had a painful picture they had to look back on. The way Jesus dealt with that picture shows how we can deal with similar pictures in our own lives.

"We live life as if it were a motion picture," said Gerald Sittser. "Loss turns life into a snapshot. The movement stops; everything freezes. We find ourselves looking at picture albums to remember the motion picture of our lives that once was but can no longer be."[1]

For Peter, the past three-and-a-half years with Christ ran through his mind like *The Greatest Story Ever Told.* But on the sprocket of one moment the film broke. And everything froze. What he was left with was a snapshot. Three snapshots actually. You'll find them mounted on the pages of Matthew's album of Christ's life.

> Now Peter was sitting outside in the courtyard, and a certain servant-girl came to him and said, "You too were with Jesus the Galilean."
>
> But he denied it before them all, saying, "I do not know what you are talking about."

And when he had gone out to the gateway, another servant-girl saw him and said to those who were there, "This man was with Jesus of Nazareth."

And again he denied it with an oath, "I do not know the man."

And a little later the bystanders came up and said to Peter, "Surely you too are one of them; for the way you talk gives you away."

Then he began to curse and swear, "I do not know the man!" And immediately a cock crowed.

And Peter remembered the word which Jesus had said, "Before a cock crows, you will deny Me three times." And he went out and wept bitterly. (26:69-75)

Peter left the courtyard with knives of remorse ripping at his soul. How could he ever face Jesus again? How could he face the others? Himself? What would he give to get those three pictures back?

THREE PICTURES OF UNDENIABLE GUILT

As you look at the pictures, you'll see that each was more intense than the one before. The first one was a sweeping dismissal. The second was more emphatic because of the oath that preceded it. The third was more emphatic still because of the cursing and swearing that punctuated it.

The three pictures came together, stopping him and revealing to him just who he was. A coward. A cringing, disloyal coward. Who would have thought? *Peter* did that? No. I can see Judas doing that, or Thomas, maybe even Philip. But *Peter?* Loyalty was his strongest trait. He was what his name said he was— a rock, one you count on, depend upon. Rain or shine, he would be there. No matter how stiff the opposition, he would be the one standing by your side. Yet he left the Savior's side under opposition as slight as a servant-girl's accusation.

Earlier in the evening, Jesus had warned him:

"Simon, Simon, behold, Satan has demanded permission to sift you like wheat; but I have prayed for you, that your faith may not fail; and you, when once you have turned again, strengthen your brothers."

And he said to Him, "Lord, with You I am ready to go both to prison and to death!"

And He said, "I say to you, Peter, the cock will not crow today until you have denied three times that you know Me." (Luke 22:31-34)

The understanding in Jesus' words show that he knew about the brokenness that was coming to Peter's life. The understanding came from a picture he had received that revealed the sledgehammer responsible for the breakage. Jesus understood that other forces were at work besides the peer pressure in the courtyard and the adrenaline pumping through Peter's heart. Working behind the scenes was Satan. Jesus, of all people, understood what it was like to withstand his blows. Three times in the wilderness he was hit with it.

Out of this understanding flowed a compassion. It was the compassion of a surgeon touching the arm of his patient right before surgery and assuring him that everything was going to be all right, that he'd be up and around in no time, back on his feet and back at work.

But the physician wasn't with the patient now. And everything wasn't all right. Everything was painful. Peter wasn't sure he'd *ever* recover. But he *was* sure he'd never be back on his feet and back to work.

What do you do with pictures like those? What do you do to get rid of the guilt, the shame, the regret? What do you do to get a few hours of relief from the pain? Peter tried getting relief the same way I tried—with activity. Take a look at the picture from a page in John's gospel.

After these things Jesus manifested Himself again to the disciples at the Sea of Tiberias, and He manifested Himself in this way. There were together Simon Peter, and Thomas called Didymus, and Nathanael of Cana in Galilee, and the sons of Zebedee, and two others of His disciples. Simon Peter said to them, "I am going fishing."

They said to him, "We will also come with you."

They went out, and got into the boat; and that night they caught nothing. (21:1-3)

Peter was trying to get his mind off the tragic events of the past few days. But he couldn't because he was rehearsing his regrets. *If only I had fought it out in the garden. That's what I should have done. Why did I put away that sword? Why? If only I hadn't gone to that courtyard. What was I thinking? Why didn't I just admit it? Yes, I know him. I'm one of his disciples. What would they have done? Lock me up, beat me, kill me? Better that torture than this.*

No, Peter wasn't getting any relief from the pain. Gerald Sittser explains why. "Regret keeps the wounds of loss from healing, putting us in a perpetual state of guilt. We think there is no forgiveness or redemption because we are deprived of the opportunity to right our wrongs."[2]

Peter knew he could never take back those pictures. He could never even apologize for the pictures. The only person who could forgive him was gone. Yes, he had returned from the dead, but he hadn't returned to Peter. And who could blame Jesus for not returning? Would *you* come back to a friend who had denied your friendship at the very time you needed it most? Would *you* come back to someone who had told you to your face he'd be there for you but behind your back had denied even knowing you?

Peter, along with James and John, comprised the inner circle of disciples. They were the ones Jesus took with him to the Mount of Transfiguration where they were given the most stunning picture of his divinity. They were also the ones he took with him to the garden of Gethsemane, where they were given the most sublime picture of his humanity. A special bond existed between them.

In his book *Forgive & Forget,* Lewis Smedes talks about the breech that disloyalty creates in that type of relationship: "Most of us have several circles of people to whom we belong by personal bonds of loyalty. Inside the circle we are bonded to each other by a promise we have made to stay at each other's side. . . . A person who breaks a promise of loyalty violates a relationship based on promise and trust. We cannot go on as usual in the relationship unless the wrong of it is healed."[3]

TWO UNFORGETTABLE PICTURES OF BLESSING

Peter couldn't go forward in his relationship with Jesus until first he went backward. Jesus knew this and orchestrated the circumstances that would bring him back. The scene is recorded in the gospel of John.

> But when the day was now breaking, Jesus stood on the beach; yet the disciples did not know that it was Jesus. Jesus therefore said to them, "Children, you do not have any fish, do you?"
>
> They answered him, "No."
>
> And He said to them, "Cast the net on the right-hand side of the boat, and you will find a catch."
>
> They cast therefore, and then they were not able to haul it in because of the great number of fish. (21:4-6)

Do you see what Jesus was doing? He was bringing back a picture from their past. A picture that had significance to all of them but especially to Peter. Page back to the early part of Luke, and you'll understand why.

> Now it came about that while the multitude were pressing around Him and listening to the word of God, He was standing by the lake of Gennesaret; and He saw two boats lying at the edge of the lake; but the fishermen had gotten out of them, and were washing their nets. And He got into one of the boats, which was Simon's, and asked him to put out a little way from the land. And He sat down and began teaching the multitudes from the boat.
>
> And when He had finished speaking, He said to Simon, "Put out into the deep water and let down your nets for a catch."
>
> And Simon answered and said, "Master, we worked hard all night and caught nothing, but at Your bidding I will let down the nets."
>
> And when they had done this, they enclosed a great quantity of fish; and their nets began to break; and they signaled to their partners in the other boat, for them to come and help them. And they came, and filled both of the boats, so that they began to sink.

But when Simon Peter saw that, he fell down at Jesus' feet, saying, "Depart from me, for I am a sinful man, O Lord!"

For amazement had seized him and all his companions because of the catch of fish which they had taken; and so also James and John, sons of Zebedee, who were partners with Simon.

And Jesus said to Simon, "Do not fear, from now on you will be catching men."

And when they had brought their boats to land, they left everything and followed Him. (5:1-11)

Of all the pictures Jesus had given him, I believe this was the one Peter treasured most. In this picture Peter first saw Jesus in a different light. In that light Peter saw something else. His sin. And knowing that Jesus saw it too made Jesus' words even more incredible. Jesus was willing to accept Peter, in spite of his sin. And not only to accept him but to commission him. It's a picture Peter never forgot. He framed it in his memory the same way I framed that moment in the movie theater when I realized Jesus was calling me, in spite of my sin, to follow him, to love him, to learn from him, to serve him.

When that picture, which was so dear to the disciples, flashed across John's mind, his mind made a connection.

That disciple therefore whom Jesus loved said to Peter, "It is the Lord."

And so when Simon Peter heard that it was the Lord, he put his outer garment on (for he was stripped for work), and threw himself into the sea. But the other disciples came in the little boat, for they were not far from the land, but about one hundred yards away, dragging the net full of fish. And so when they got out upon the land, they saw a charcoal fire already laid, and fish placed on it, and bread.

Jesus said to them, "Bring some of the fish which you have now caught."

Simon Peter went up, and drew the net to land, full of large fish, a hundred and fifty-three; and although there were so many, the net was not torn.

Jesus said to them, "Come and have breakfast." None of the disciples ventured to question Him, "Who are You?" knowing that it was the Lord.

Jesus came and took the bread, and gave them, and the fish likewise. (John 21:7-13)

A closer look at the scene reveals that Jesus set the stage to bring back another picture to Peter's mind. There are only two places in the entire New Testament where the word *charcoal* is used. Here in verse 9 and a few chapters earlier in John 18:18.

Now the slaves and the officers were standing there, having made a *charcoal* fire, for it was cold and they were warming themselves; and Peter also was with them, standing and warming himself.

The same type of fire that warmed Peter now had also warmed him the night of his denial. What thoughts must have been shivering through Peter's mind as he stood there, dripping wet, warming himself by that fire? Whatever they were, he kept them to himself, for there is no mention of any words passing between him and Jesus.

The silence around the fire, mingled with the smells of fish and bread, I'm sure evoked another picture. The picture of Jesus feeding the five thousand. And with the picture the caption: "I am the bread of life. He who comes to me shall never hunger."

How Peter hungered for that bread. How he hungered to have again the bond that once existed between them. But how could he? How could ever get back what he had lost in that evening of disloyalty? After Jesus fed the disciples, he turned to satisfy the deeper hunger in Peter's life.

So when they had finished breakfast, Jesus said to Simon Peter, "Simon, son of John, do you love Me more than these?"

He said to Him, "Yes, Lord; You know that I love You."

He said to him, "Tend My lambs."

He said to him again a second time, "Simon, son of John, do you love Me?"

He said to Him, "Yes, Lord; You know that I love You."

He said to him, "Shepherd My sheep."

He said to him the third time, "Simon, son of John, do you love Me?"

Peter was grieved because He said to him the third time, "Do you love Me?" And he said to Him, "Lord, You know all things; You know that I love You."

Jesus said to him, "Tend My sheep. Truly, truly, I say to you, when you were younger, you used to gird yourself, and walk wherever you wished; but when you grow old, you will stretch out your hands, and someone else will gird you, and bring you where you do not wish to go."

Now this He said, signifying by what kind of death he would glorify God. And when He had spoken this, He said to him, "Follow Me!" (John 21:15-19)

Ever so gently, like a surgeon taking shrapnel out of a soldier's wounded heart, Jesus was bringing back those painful pictures. Three times he probed the wound. One time for each denial. I think it did Peter good just to talk to Jesus again, just to look in his eyes, hear the tenderness in his voice. I think it did him good to tell Jesus he still loved him. But I also think it grieved him that Jesus kept pressing him about it.

Peter's attention was on what Jesus said, but look at what Jesus could have said but didn't. He didn't say, "Okay, what do you have to say for yourself?" He didn't say, "How *could* you?" He didn't say, "And you call yourself *a Christian*?" He didn't say, "Some friend *you* turned out to be." He didn't say, "I'm so disappointed in you" or "I was wrong about you" or "You're through, finished; it's over."

JESUS REFRAMED THE PICTURES

What Jesus did say in essence was, "I still want you, I still need you, I still think you're the right person for the job." In between the lines of Jesus' words is forgiveness. Ironically, it was Peter who had such a hard time forgiving. It was he who asked Jesus, "How often shall my brother sin against me and I forgive him? Up to seven times?" To which Jesus replied, "I do not say to you up to seven times, but up to seventy times seven" (Matthew 18:21-22). Which is another way of saying indefinitely. Paul put it this way, "Love . . . does not take into account a wrong suffered" (1 Corinthians 13:5). Love and forgiveness go hand in hand. Peter needed to learn that. That morning on the beach he did.

On that beach Jesus brought back certain pictures from Peter's past. Some were precious, like his decision to become a disciple. Some were painful, like his denial. All of them were brought to Peter's mind not for his humiliation but for his healing.

The picture of Peter's denial was painful not only to him but to Jesus. After all, *Jesus* was the one who was denied. He could have gone to heaven without ever looking back at that painful moment.

Instead, he stayed to pick up the pictures.

He stooped down to pick *this* one out of the dirt.

Jesus turned and looked at Peter the very moment of his last denial (Luke 22:61). The picture was sharp and clear. And he chose to remember it. But the way Jesus remembered it is important. He brought understanding to the picture by restoring a part of it that wasn't visible to the naked eye. That was the part about Satan's involvement in Peter's denial (Luke 22:31). Then Jesus retinted the picture with compassion, telling Peter he had prayed for him (Luke 22:32). Next, Jesus reframed the picture by forgiving Peter (John 21:1-23). And finally, he revered the picture by placing it on a wall of honor in the Scriptures.

The choice Jesus made brought the healing Peter needed to go forward. And maybe it was something Jesus needed, too, before he would go forward to be with the Father.

Stories celebrate our freedom to choose—to be characters—a wonderful, terrible freedom that makes it possible for things to be different.

Daniel Taylor

The Healing Power of Stories

The Unfinished Business of the Past

There is a story of a young rabbi who was eager for recognition from the village in which he lived. He was convinced he was wise and worthy of respect, but for some reason he couldn't convince the villagers. As a result, he became bitter and vengeful.

He seized the opportunity for vengeance one day when an old, wise, and respected rabbi visited the village. He devised a test. He would put a small bird in the palm of his hand and ask the old rabbi if the bird were alive or dead. If the rabbi said "alive," he would crush the bird to death and display it for all to see. If the rabbi said "dead," he would open his hand and let the bird fly away. Surely with this test, he thought, he would get the recognition and respect he deserved.

The next day while the older rabbi was sitting among the villagers, the younger rabbi challenged him. "Rabbi, we all know how wise you are, but can you answer this? Is the bird in my hand dead or alive?"

The rabbi was silent. Then with kindness in his eyes, he looked into the eyes of the younger rabbi. "It is up to you, my friend. It is up to you."

The same is true for you and me. What we do with the pictures in our hands is up to us. To bring life or death to those pictures is up to us. To bring light or darkness to them is up to us. To bring a blessing or a curse to them is up to us. We can do with the pictures what we please. We can keep them boxed away in the attic, or we can take them down and try to see the story the pictures tell. We can curse the past like victims of circumstance, or we can bless it like victors *over* our circumstances. It's up to us. It's our choice.

In some of the strongest and most compelling stories, the main character makes life-and-death choices. These choices give the story energy. They make the plot intriguing. They also change the character. The character who doesn't make choices is weak and passive. So if we want our lives to tell strong and compelling stories in which the characters grow into people of blessing, then we—the characters—have to make choices. Choices that are sometimes difficult. Choices that are sometimes painful. Choices that are sometimes critical, where something important is at stake.

Even as we make choices regarding which pictures we're going to live by, there is another choice we have to make.

What to do with the *other* pictures.

Although we don't live by them, we are still left with them. And although we may want to leave the pictures in the past, we rarely can because they seldom stay there. "In one sense the past is dead and gone, never to be repeated, over and done with," says Frederick Buechner, "but in another sense, it is of course not done with at all or at least not done with us."[1]

Ignoring those pictures doesn't make them go away. We can put them in the closet, turn off the light, lock the door, throw away the key. But they're still there, as Larry Crabb reminds us.

Most of us have memories we won't think about—painful moments with a parent that may seem trivial till we reflect on them, wrenching episodes of sexual or emotional abuse. Ignoring past pain sometimes seems like the only logical thing to do, yet pockets of angry rage stay hidden in our soul. To deny we're hungry after days without food and that we feel angry toward people who could have fed us but refused is not evidence of maturity. Christians starving during a famine feel just as hungry as unfed pagans. It's right to admit we're hungry and normal to look for food to satisfy us.[2]

The first choice we need to make in dealing with those kinds of pictures is to admit our hunger. It is a step of awareness, of remembrance.

CHOOSING TO REMEMBER THE PICTURES

The theme of remembrance is woven throughout the Bible. Remember God's commandments, said Moses (Numbers 15:39). Remember God's wonders, said the psalmist (Psalm 105:5). Remember the Creator in the days of your youth, said Solomon (Ecclesiastes 12:1).

Just as the thread of remembrance is stitched throughout the fabric of the Scriptures, so is the darker thread of forgetfulness. Lapses in memory were responsible for national as well as individual sins. The adulterous woman, said Solomon, "forgets the covenant of her God" (Proverbs 2:17). So does the adulterous nation. "And the sons of Israel did what was evil in the sight of the LORD, and forgot the LORD their God, and served the Baals and the Asheroth" (Judges 3:7).

Remembering is crucial not only in biblical history but in our personal history as well. So the first choice we must make about the pictures we're left with is to remember them. Even the ones that are difficult to remember.

Again, there is biblical precedence. Israel was told to remember their slavery in Egypt (Deuteronomy 5:15) and to remember the way God disciplined them in the wilderness (Deuteronomy 8:1-5).

But why should *we* go back and look at pictures like that in our own lives? What purpose does it serve? Why not let the past rest in peace?

Nobel Peace Prize Winner Elie Wiesel explains why he looks at pictures like that in his past. "We remember Auschwitz and all that it symbolizes because we believe that, in spite of the past and its horrors, the world is worthy of salvation; and salvation, like redemption, can only be found in memory."[3]

One of the reforms Josiah was responsible for instituting related to Israel's memory. Under Manasseh and Amon the nation had forgotten God. The price the nation paid for its forgetfulness was dear. When Josiah ascended the throne, the nation started remembering again. The first stage of their remembering started with the king's order to repair the Temple. As workmen were repairing the damage, they found a part of Israel's forgotten past. A lost copy of the book of the Law. Josiah used the discovery to help restore the nation's memory. He gathered the people of Jerusalem to the Temple and read them the book. He then made a covenant between the people and God to bring the nation into submission to his commands. One of those commands involved the celebration of Passover. A feast of remembrance. A feast associated with a painful period in the nation's past, their enslavement in Egypt.

The Christian community has a similar meal of remembrance in our celebration of the Lord's Supper. "Do this in remembrance of Me," Jesus said as he instituted the memorial in the upper room (Luke 22:19). What we are asked to remember is not a pretty picture. It is the cross. How the Savior thirsted there. How he suffered there. How he died there. And how we are to live our lives in the light of that picture.

One of the reasons we choose not to look at those pictures is fear. There's a war story that illustrates this. After World War II ended and Japan signed its peace treaties, thousands of Japanese soldiers on the outlying islands refused to surrender. They had been so brainwashed by their country as to what might happen to them at the hands of the enemy that they hid. Finally the Japanese emperor made a speech that was recorded and played over loudspeakers aimed at the caves and jungles where the soldiers were hiding: "Come out. The war is over. Peace has been established. You will not be harmed but welcomed and protected."

The troops responded to the familiar voice of their emperor and came out of their jungle caves. Within months most of the soldiers had been accounted for. As the years passed, the government assumed all of them had surrendered and returned to their homes. But in March of 1974 one last soldier came out of hiding. After twenty-nine years. A photograph of the scruffy sixty-year-old soldier appeared on magazine covers around the world. Asked why he had waited so long to come out, he said it had taken him that long to get over his fears.

Sometimes in our war with the past, fear keeps us from coming out of our cave. It's hard for us to believe the war could really be over. It's hard to believe peace is possible. It's hard to believe we won't be tortured by our enemies if we do come out.

The first step, however unsteady it may seem, starts us on a path out of the jungle of our fears and into the light of a new relationship of peace we can have with our past.

Gerald Sittser had a picture in his life that was fearful to face. It was of an accident in which three people he loved were killed by a drunk driver.

> I remember those first moments after the accident as if everything was happening in slow motion. They are frozen into my memory with a terrible vividness. After recovering my breath, I turned around to survey the damage. The scene was chaotic. I remember the look of terror on the faces of my children and the feeling of horror that swept over me when I saw the unconscious and broken bodies of Lynda, my four-year-old daughter Diana Jane, and my mother. I remember getting Catherine (then eight), David (seven), and John (two) out of the van through my door, the only one that would open. I remember taking pulses, doing mouth-to-mouth resuscitation, trying to save and calm the living. I remember the feeling of panic that struck my soul as I watched Lynda, my mother, and Diana Jane all die before my eyes. I remember the pandemonium that followed—people gawking, lights flashing from emergency vehicles, a helicopter whirring overhead, cars lining up, medical experts doing what they could do to help. And I remember the realization sweeping over me that I would soon plunge into a darkness from which I might never again emerge as a sane, normal, believing man.[4]

By not repressing those painful pictures, Sittser was able over time to find moments of grace that brought light to those dark pictures. One of the illuminating truths he discovered was the importance of the way we remember those pictures. "Our memory of the past is not neutral. It can poison us or heal us, depending on how we remember it. Remembering the wrong done can make us a prisoner to pain and hatred, or it can make us the recipient of the grace, love, and healing power of God."[5]

It's what Lewis Smedes calls *redemptive remembering*. "There is a healing way to remember the wrongs of our irreversible past, a way that can bring hope for the future along with our sorrow for the past. Redemptive remembering keeps a clear picture of the past, but it adds a new setting and shifts its focus."[6]

In order for our remembering to become redemptive, we must take a series of steps. The first is a step toward awareness, a step of choosing to remember the pictures. The second is a step toward understanding, a step of choosing to restore the pictures.

CHOOSING TO RESTORE THE PICTURES

If part of a photograph has been torn off or if a spot has obscured part of it, we can take it to a photography studio to be restored. It may not look as perfect as the original once did, but the specialist can often fill in enough of the missing information to make the photograph much clearer.

The decision to restore the pictures of the past is a step toward understanding the parts that are missing or obscured.

It's much easier to respond to a curse with a blessing if we have some understanding of why the other person acted the way he or she did. If a child throws a temper tantrum when he comes home from school, running off to his room and shouting that he hates us, we can deal more easily with the situation if we understand what might have happened during the day to cause him to respond like that. If we look beyond his hateful words, maybe we find that earlier in the day someone threw hateful words at him, or he was shamed by a teacher, or he was made fun of for having a crush on one of the girls in his class, and he bottled those feelings inside until he came home. These things don't excuse his actions, but they do help us to understand them.

To help bus drivers understand the actions of the passengers that made them angry, New York City came up with an ingenious program. They filmed the passengers. The only perspective the bus driver had of the passengers was from his overhead mirror, and then it was only a glance. The film gave another perspective, revealing that a passenger wasn't drunk, as the driver had supposed, but was really an epileptic. Another passenger who the driver thought was rude was really mentally ill. Having this understanding helped the drivers cope. For example, if someone repeatedly pulled the bell for the bus to stop, the driver's first thought was not that the passenger was being rude but that he was probably an anxious person, maybe even a handicapped person, fearful of missing his stop.

Seeing the broader picture instead of the limited perspective from our rearview mirror brings light to the narrow pictures. Joseph's story is a good example. He was sold by his brothers to an Egyptian caravan. Can you imagine how painful that was to look back on? Sold by your own brothers. In Egypt, Joseph rose to prominence within Pharaoh's court, only to be throw in prison when he refused the sexual advances of Potiphar's wife. Look at the pictures that could have haunted him while he was in prison. The picture of his being sold into slavery because of his brothers' jealousy. The picture of his being thrown into prison because he refused to sin against God and sleep with his employer's wife.

While in prison Joseph interpreted the dreams of Pharaoh's baker and cupbearer. When Pharaoh learned of Joseph's gift, he released him and appointed him chief of state, responsible for overseeing all of his affairs. Years later, because of his position, Joseph was able to save his own family from the ravages of famine when they came to Egypt seeking food. When Joseph's brothers recognized him, they were afraid he would respond in kind, returning the evil they had done to him. They trembled and fell down before him. Joseph's response?

> "Do not be afraid, for am I in God's place? And as for you, you meant evil against me, but God meant it for good in order to bring about this present result, to preserve many people alive. So therefore, do not be afraid; I will provide for you and your little ones." So he comforted them and spoke kindly to them. (Genesis 50:19-21)

What a beautiful way to deal with a painful picture from the past! He could do it, I think, because he placed the picture of what his brothers had done within the bigger picture of God's plan for the world. But sometimes the bigger picture isn't as easy to see as it was for Joseph. Take Gerald Sittser's case, for example. He never understood why he lost three members of his family to a drunk driver, but he knew it was important to try to understand.

> I have imagined my own story fitting into some greater scheme, the half of which I may never fathom. I simply do not see the bigger picture, but *I choose to believe* that there is a bigger picture and that my loss is part of some wonderful story authored by God himself. Sometimes I wonder about how my own experience of loss will someday serve a greater purpose that I do not yet see or understand. My story may help to redeem a bad past, or it may bring about a better future. Perhaps my own family heritage has produced generations of absent and selfish fathers, and I have been given a chance to reverse that pattern. Perhaps people suffering catastrophic loss will someday look to our family for hope and inspiration. I do not know. Yet I choose to believe that God is working toward some ultimate purpose, even using my loss to that end.[7]

When we choose to bring understanding to the pictures of our past, something happens that changes them in our eyes. Which brings us to the next step in bringing life and light to *all* our relationships.

CHOOSING TO RETINT THE PICTURES

Retinting photographs is an old technique that became popular in the days when only black-and-white film was available. People would brush color onto the pictures to make them look more lifelike, adding a little brown to the hair, a little blush to the cheeks, a little blue to the eyes. The effect humanizes the picture.

The effect of adding color to black-and-white pictures found its way into moving pictures too. In the 1927 Cecil B. DeMille version of *The King of*

Kings, color was used in only two of the film's fourteen reels, at the beginning of the movie and at the end. The effect evoked greater feeling from the audience, particularly as they watched the crucifixion.

A similar technique was used more recently in the film *Schindler's List.* With the exception of a short segment at the beginning and end of the movie, the film is shot entirely in black and white, giving it the archival feel of an old documentary. The only other color in the film is the retinting of a little girl's coat. We see her in several short scenes, dressed in a lightly tinted, reddish coat. We see her first in a crowd scene, where she would have gone unnoticed without the tinting. We see her again, this time under a bed where she is hiding from the Nazis. The last time we see that tinted red coat is on a conveyor belt of dead bodies being dumped into a mass grave. We see only the briefest glimpses of the little girl, but amid the somber collection of grays the other people are wearing, she stands out. The tinting of the coat makes her seem somehow more human. Which makes us feel something for her we didn't feel for the other people, other people who were just as human but who didn't have a tinted coat.

The retinting of the picture made us feel compassion. *Compassion* comes from the Latin root *pati,* meaning "to feel" or "to suffer," and the prefix *com,* meaning "with." When we have compassion on people, we feel something of their pain, we take something of their suffering inside us and suffer with them.

Our compassion for people is often in proportion to our understanding of them. David said that God has compassion on us like a father has on his children (Psalm 103:13). Why? David gave the reason in the next verse, "For He Himself knows our frame; He is mindful that we are but dust" (v. 14).

When Jesus looked at Peter at the moment of his denial, he felt compassion for the disciple. He knew the circumstances in the spiritual realm that contributed to Peter's failure. Seeing that part of the bigger picture, Jesus could more easily look at him with compassion and pray for him.

In his book *Legacy of the Heart: The Spiritual Advantages of a Painful Childhood,* Wayne Muller helps us to see that retinting the pictures of the past is a choice.

Each childhood wound and every spiritual teaching has been presented to help us cultivate a particular aspect of mercy and compassion toward ourselves. At each juncture we have been confronted with a choice: Do we meet ourselves and our wounds with judgment or with mercy? Do we touch our childhood memories with anger, or soften them with love and forgiveness? Do we recall our violations with shame, or embrace them with genuine acceptance; do we react with fear and isolation, or with faith and courage? Do we add to the violence within ourselves, or do we cultivate unconditional love and kindness for all we have been and all we have become?[8]

We see a touching example of this in a story Gerald Sittser relates about his seven-year-old son's response to the drunk driver who killed his mother, sister, and grandmother. It was long past bedtime when he crawled up on his father's lap, sitting for a while in silence. Then out came the tears and the confusion and the anger at the man who had hurt him so deeply by taking away his loved ones. He wanted to make the man hurt, too, wanted to make the whole world hurt the way he hurt. He just sat there and cried until the tears and the anger had run their course. After the tears had dried, he said something so poignant. "You know, Dad, I bet someone hurt him, too, like maybe his parents. That's why he did something to hurt us. And then I bet someone else hurt his parents. It just keeps going on and on. When will it ever stop?"[9]

It will stop when we decide to bring light to those pictures instead of adding to the darkness. It will stop when we decide to bring life to those relationships instead of contributing to the death of those relationships. For it to stop, we must choose mercy instead of judgment, love instead of hate, compassion instead of indifference. The blessing instead of a curse.

But compassion, as strong a feeling as it is, is still simply a feeling. If our remembering is to be redemptive, we need to go beyond feelings. As Jesus did with Peter, we must reframe the pictures.

CHOOSING TO REFRAME THE PICTURES

It's amazing the difference reframing can make to a picture. If we crop off part of the picture, it may change the center of interest. If we use the right matting, it brings out colors in the picture that were so subtle we didn't notice them before. If we use a different frame, it may enhance the picture, making it seem deeper and richer.

Reframing a picture causes us to look at it differently. The same is true with pictures from our past. The new frame is forgiveness. We see it used time and time again in the Bible.

David was Israel's greatest king, yet he committed adultery and then premeditated murder to cover it up. But when the New Testament looks back on David's life, it crops those things from the picture, calling him a man after God's own heart (Acts 13:22). The same is true of Abraham. He had many failings of faith. His tryst with Hagar to hurry along God's promise. His pawning off Sarah as his sister to save his own skin. And yet when the New Testament puts a frame around his life, it is matted to bring out the triumphs of his faith not his failures (Romans 4:18-21). Turning to the gallery of faith in Hebrews 11, we see pictures of a lot of flawed people: Noah, Moses, Jacob, Samson. Although we could focus on a lot of shameful things in each of their lives, the writer to the Hebrews chose to focus on their faith. That is the way of grace. When it looks back, it is with a forgiving eye.

Lewis Smedes, in his book *Forgive & Forget,* explains why it is so important to look back at the pictures in our past with such an eye . . . and what happens when we don't.

> Recall the pain of being wronged, the hurt of being stung, cheated, demeaned. Doesn't the memory of it fuel the fire of fury again, reheat the pain again, make it hurt again? Suppose you never forgive, suppose you feel the hurt each time your memory lights on the people who did you wrong. And suppose you have a compulsion to think of them constantly. You have become a prisoner of your past pain; you are locked into a torture chamber

of your own making. Time should have left your pain behind; but you keep it alive to let it flay at you over and over.

Your own memory is a replay of your hurt—a videotape within your soul that plays unending reruns of your old rendezvous with pain. You cannot switch it off. You are hooked into it like a pain junkie; you become addicted to your remembrance of pain past. You are lashed again each time your memory spins the tape. Is this fair to yourself—this wretched justice of not forgiving? You could not be more unfair to yourself.

The only way to heal the pain that will not heal itself is to forgive the person who hurt you. Forgiving stops the reruns of pain. Forgiving heals your memory as you change your memory's vision.[10]

Again, it's a choice. We can't choose the hurt that comes into our lives, but we can choose how we will respond to that hurt. George Macdonald, the Scottish storyteller whose writings had an enormous effect on C. S. Lewis, said a sobering thing about the significance of that choice: "It may be infinitely worse to refuse to forgive than to murder, because the latter may be an impulse of a moment of heat, whereas the former is a cold and deliberate choice of the heart."

Forgiveness alters the way we look at the people in our past who have hurt us. Some would argue that once we forgive, we should forget. There is some value to that, but there is a greater value, I think, in keeping some remembrance of the past before us for further reflection. Which brings us to the final step in the process.

CHOOSING TO REVERE THE PICTURES

Once we've gone through all the trouble it takes to remember, restore, retint, and reframe the pictures in our lives, it makes little sense to turn around and store them in the basement. There should be a place somewhere to display them. Some place where they can be seen in a new light . . . and in the overall context of the story God is telling with your life.

The pictures of the past are, after all, a part of your life, a record of where you've been and who you've met along the way and how you've changed as a result. The pictures are a photo album that tells something about who you are, why you feel as you do about certain things, why you react the way you do, why you cry at some things and don't at others, what are your hopes, your fears, your dreams, your passions.

It's important in some way to keep the past before you as part of an on-going conversation, giving thanks for what was good, extending forgiveness for what wasn't, praying for understanding, waiting for compassion to come. The unfinished business of the past isn't a clerical procedure where papers are signed and dated and notarized in one transaction. It takes time. And the deeper the hurt, the longer it often takes.

Most of us forgive in steps. Instead of making one sweeping judicial pardon, we usually forgive specifics as they come to our minds. That's why it's important to keep that reframed picture before us. It helps us to grow in our understanding as new pieces of information may cause us to see the picture differently. And as we grow in our understanding, we will grow in our capacity to feel compassion, which will lead us into fuller expressions of forgiveness.

The wilderness was a painful set of pictures for the nation of Israel to look back on. People hungered there, thirsted there, died there. It was a place of shame, for it was their unbelief that led them there and kept them there for so long. Yet they were told to remember the pictures but to remember them in a different light than in the days when all they saw was the lack of food and the desolation of the desert.

"And you shall remember all the way which the LORD your God has led you in the wilderness these forty years. . . . He led you through the great and terrible wilderness, with its fiery serpents and scorpions and thirsty ground where there was no water; He brought water for you out of the rock of flint. In the wilderness He fed you manna which your fathers did not know, that He might humble you and that He might test you, to do good for you in the end" (Deuteronomy 8:2,15-16).

Understanding where God was in those pictures made a huge difference in how they looked back on them. The same is true for us.

As we come to the New Testament, we see that those pictures have been passed down to the generations that followed. A place of remembrance has been set aside for those pictures. In talking about Israel's failings in the wilderness, Paul said, "Now these things happened as examples for us, that we should not crave evil things, as they also craved. And do not be idolaters, as some of them were; as it is written, 'The people sat down to eat and drink, and stood up to play.' Nor let us act immorally, as some of them did, and twenty-three thousand fell in one day. Nor let us try the Lord, as some of them did, and were destroyed by the serpents. Nor grumble, as some of them did, and were destroyed by the destroyer. Now these things happened to them as an example, and they were written for our instruction" (1 Corinthians 10:6-11).

We revere the new pictures that have been reframed by putting them in a place of honor, some place where they can remind us of who God is and how he has worked in our lives. It's a way of honoring him for the good he has brought forth from the pain of our past, something of a visual aid to Romans 8:28. And it's a motivating form of instruction, as Paul used it, for the continuing education of our faith.

This memorial with its wall of names, becomes a place of quiet reflection, and a tribute to those who served their nation in difficult times. All who come here can find it a place of healing.

From a report to the Vietnam Veterans Memorial Fund

announcing the winning design for the memorial,

Always to Remember by Brent Ashabranner

The Beginning of the End Is Remembrance

While studying at American University, Vietnam veteran Jan Scruggs came up with the idea that America needed some kind of memorial to the men and women who had died in Vietnam. But it wasn't until two years later, in 1979, that the idea took hold of him. One evening he saw the movie *The Deer Hunter,* and it bothered him so much he couldn't sleep. He tossed and turned all night with flashbacks of his own combat experiences, horrible memories of a mortar attack that left twelve of his friends dead. The next morning he told his wife he was going to build a memorial, and all the names of the dead would be on it. That was his vision.

He made phone calls, wrote letters, did research, and went to Washington. His vision grew into an obsession. He sold a piece of land to start a fund—the Vietnam Veteran's Memorial Fund. He solicited funds, lobbied Congress, selected a board of directors, and finally was successful in getting the official go-ahead to take submissions for its design.

By the design deadline, the Fund had received 1,421 submissions, more than any other design competition in the history of the country. Scruggs insisted on only one design element: The memorial had to have the name of every man and woman killed or missing in the war. The winner of the competition was Maya Ying Lin, a twenty-one-year-old student at Yale. No one had ever heard of this Chinese-American girl, yet she beat out some of the best-known names in American art and architecture.

Her design consisted of two walls, made of highly polished black granite, in a wide V-shape, the east wall pointing to the Lincoln Memorial, the west wall pointing to the Washington Monument. She had chosen black granite partly because of its reflective quality to give back images of the people who visited it as well as reflections of the trees, the sky, and grass.

Despite the controversy surrounding the memorial, when it was dedicated, an amazing thing happened. One by one, as people began spotting the names of their loved ones, they reached out their hands to touch them. People started taking off their gloves, fingers straining to touch the etchings, evoking powerful memories. People wept. People embraced. People talked and prayed. After two decades of silence, the pain and anguish began to spill from America's soul. And that day, the nation's wound began to heal.

An interesting phenomenon resulted. People started bringing mementos to the wall and leaving them. They brought so many that a warehouse had to be used to store them all. About a third of the mementos are military in nature: ribbons, medals, identification tags. About a third are written material, cards, letters, poems. The other third is a miscellaneous category of toys, books, phonograph records. Each item is given an inventory number along with the number of the panel on the wall where it was found.

The curator of these mementos is a man named David Guynes. When asked why they save all those things, he opened a cabinet full of toys and took out a small, worn teddy bear. "This was one of the early mementos left at the memorial," he said. "A mother and father whose son's name is on the wall put it there. They left a greeting card, too, and a photograph of a 1955 car. Newspaper articles were written about the bear, and the parents identified themselves. They were interviewed on Ted Koppel's *Nightline* television program. They said they had bought the bear for their son in 1938 when he was a baby. They wanted to return it to him. The car in the photo was his first car. . . . Most museums, most curators, carefully select what is to make up their collection," he said. "That's not the case here. We must collect everything. There are so many questions, so many mysteries, in these memorabilia. So many stories are in them, so much feeling, emotion, heartache. What can be learned about America and Americans from these things they have brought? Altogether, these materials make up a very important part of the story of Vietnam."[1]

My name might have been on that wall had I not heard the stories my dad told one night about his days in the war. In the *Winds of War*, Herman Wouk wrote that "the beginning of the end of war is in remembrance." That was true for all the Vietnam veterans who had come back from the war but who were still living with it, still sleeping with it, still fighting it, still trying to drink it or drug it away. For many of them, the memorial was the beginning of the end of the war that had raged inside them with such intensity and had mounted such staggering losses.

AN UNEXPECTED GIFT

The war that waged within me was less intense, but still there were losses and pain. Some of the pain was eased when I was away at college. I attended Texas Christian University in Ft. Worth, Texas, but this particular day I drove to Southern Methodist University in Dallas to do some research in their library. While I was there, I saw a sign on the door that stopped me: "Robert M. Trent—Head Librarian." To this day I don't know why I did it, but I popped my head in his door and said, "Hey, Uncle Bob. I'm your long-lost nephew, John Trent."

He sat back in his chair, suddenly alert, and asked, "Where are you from?"

"Phoenix."

"Are you Joe's boy?"

My mouth dropped open. I couldn't believe it. He *was* my Uncle Bob, actually my dad's uncle, which made him my great-uncle. He invited me home for dinner, and there he restored some of the missing parts of my dad's picture. There were five brothers in all, he told me. And they had all grown up on a farm, working from the time they got up in the morning until the time they went to bed. None of them were close to their dad, who looked at them more as hired hands than sons. Several of them had gone to war. He talked about my dad's experiences in the war . . . how the first two or three years he was back he had nightmares . . . how he self-medicated with alcohol.

I had chosen to remember my dad, not to blot him from my past, but that night at my great-uncle's house wasn't a choice I made so much as a gift I received. A gift of understanding. And from that understanding came the first feelings of compassion. I felt something for him, something of the ache he must have had for the dad he never really knew, something of the torment that wouldn't let him rest, something of the sorrows he carried within him that he tried to wash out of his system with alcohol. Suddenly the picture I had of him in my mind changed. It was no longer a black-and-white photograph that was showing its age with sepia. I had retinted it somehow in my mind, humanizing it with color.

I had forgiven him, I think, at least the best I could for where I was and who I was. But forgiving wasn't easy. And it didn't come all at once. The night at my great-uncle's helped. So did the memorial.

A SHADOWBOX OF HONOR

I made it years later. It was a shadowbox. I filled it with the few mementos I had. The soldier's cap he wore. The medals and ribbons he received. A few things like that. I made it because I wanted to honor what I could, in truth, really honor about his life. This was my wall. This is where I touched the past. And this is where I received a measure, at least, of healing.

Down the way from the Vietnam Veteran's Memorial is the Lincoln Memorial. Engraved on it are the words of his Second Inaugural Address to the nation. The final words of the address are:

> With malice toward none, with charity for all, with firmness in the
> right as God gives us to see the right, let us finish the work we are
> in, to bind up the nation's wounds, to care for him who shall have
> borne the battle, and for his widow and his orphans, and to do all

which may achieve and cherish a just and a lasting peace among ourselves and with all nations.

The nation's wounds. The soldiers who have borne the battle. The widows of war. The orphans of war. Gettysburg. Vietnam. Guadalcanal. A dark and empty football field.

"The beginning of the end of war is remembrance."

A documentary remembering the Civil War aired sometime ago on PBS. It was produced by Ken Burns, who combined old photographs, personal letters, and a wonderful weave of narrations that brought the past to life. When you heard volley after volley of rifle fire at the Battle of Gettysburg, for example, you began to sense the toll of human life that was taken. After a while you wanted to shout at them to stop the shooting, to stop the killing, to put down their rifles. Of course you couldn't, and so the killing continued until this, the bloodiest battle of the Civil War, was over. On the fiftieth anniversary of the battle, there was a reunion of the veterans who had fought there. Somebody had the idea, almost a boyish idea, to recreate the scene of Pickett's charge. The Union soldiers took their place on the ridge. The Confederate soldiers took their place on the field. Someone sounded the charge, and the Union soldiers came out of hiding, running toward the Confederates. Before they reached each other, though, something incredible happened. The whoops and hollers turned to tears. And when they collided on that field, they fell into each other's arms, weeping.

My remembrance of the war I fought is a shadowbox. I placed it in our home, above the piano where Kari and Laura practice. He hadn't been a hero in my life or my children's lives. But he had been a hero for our country. For that I give him the honor that is due him. And to make peace, the best I could, with my past.

The pictures we're left with. Have you made peace with your pictures yet?

PART 2

The Pictures We're Blessed With

HAVE YOU EVER had a mechanic explain a car repair to you . . . and not understood a single term or recognized the name of a much-needed part? You see him nod urgently and hear the words come out. It *sounds* important. And you know there's a genuine problem with the rattle or screech that brought you in. But his solution invites you into a world of automotive technology and terms as easily understood as Romanian or Hutu.

For me the worst thing about that situation is knowing I have to *trust* that person. Someone I don't know. Someone who might give excellent service or could be cannon fodder for the next *60 Minutes* exposé. Someone who aside from the overalls and grease-stained fingernails could be a refrigerator salesman *dressed up* as a mechanic!

Without really understanding, I have to trust everything from his first estimate to whether I can drive away one day without coming back the next.

I fear that talking and writing about blessing others can usher in a similar fear or applicational amnesia. We know it's an important word. After all, it's used in the Scriptures more than three hundred times. We sing about it. Read it in our church bulletins and our Christmas cards. Hear it discussed regularly on Christian radio and in sermons. We may even know that our kids need it.

But we also bless people when they sneeze. Some of us have had the experience of being blessed out. We get a tax refund and count it a blessing. In a fallen world which muddies the meaning of many important words, the word *blessing* can become an important sounding term—like hydraulic line capacitor—but we don't have a clue as to what it is.

In the case of the blessing, however, there's no need to nod knowingly (even when we don't know) and walk away with our fingers crossed.

When it comes to understanding how to live out the blessing, we have something far better than any service guarantee or sales manager's word of honor. We have a guarantee based on the fact that God's Word is dependable. Truthful. Always consistent. Never changing. When it speaks on a subject like the blessing, it's a real estimate of what's at stake and of the benefits and costs involved. I feel that's the main reason *The Gift of the Blessing* has remained popular for more than a decade.

When I first looked at that biblical concept, brought to life in the story of Jacob and Esau, I saw five tangible specifics from the Scriptures that a parent could use to bless each child.

God's Word—linked with that picture—suddenly made the concept of blessing more tangible. More accessible. More easily in reach for us everyday Janes and Joes. A hammer or screwdriver instead of a bearing liner or brake shoe.

After looking at the blessing pictured in Genesis, at least I knew that hugging and holding my child appropriately, from the earliest age, passed on love without words.

Then there were the words of love themselves . . . whether spoken . . . written . . . calligraphed . . . e-mailed . . . whispered. Audible expressions that could be treasured and reproduced in a listener's heart. The kinds of words that end the guessing game far too many grown children are forced to play. ("I know they loved me . . . *at least I think so.* . . . But if only I could have heard it—even once.")

Attaching high value was another part of the parental blessing, which means attaching God's value to our children. Over things and schedules. Over careers and our own convenience. A choice to make little lives and needs a priority not an inconvenience.

Linked with it was how blessing others pictured a special future. Encouraging our children to live up to who they can become in Christ instead of living down to a curse.

Finally, the parental blessing ended with a focus on "genuine commitment," which is where this section of the book begins.

As we live out the blessing every day, there's nothing wrong with looking at that short, five-part list of affirming words and actions. But it's one thing to apply them with our children and quite another at work or at the ball game or in line at the grocery store. (Try to "appropriately hug or touch" people the next time you're at the bank, and you'll probably get arrested!)

How then do you bless everyday people? A spouse? Even strangers?

To live out the blessing with others, we need more than just the picture of a loving parent. We need other pictures. And the Scriptures give us a number of pictures that show us what it means to bless another and how.

I'm convinced the Lord knew we needed pictures of what it means to bless. And if looking at a "picture" of Jacob and Esau could make the parental blessing more tangible—more everyday—then looking at pictures of how Christ, the one who loved people most of all, gave the blessing to others will help us do the same.

That's why in this section we'll look at the pictures we're blessed with. Especially the pictures of how Christ blessed others. Then we'll drop our eyes to two pictures of prominent people (each a princess in her own way) and finally to two parents (my own). All of these are living lessons of people who chose to live out—or not to live out—those biblical pictures of blessing.

It's my prayer that you'll find the right pictures—actually the right *source* of positive pictures—that can leave you saying, "The blessing. Now I understand!"

Remember those moments in our own lives when with only the dullest understanding but with the sharpest longing we have glimpsed that Christ's kind of life is the only life that matters and that all other kinds of life are riddled with death; remember the moments in our lives when Christ came to us in countless disguises through people who one way or another strengthened us, comforted us, healed us, judged us, by the power of Christ within them. All that is the past. All that is what there is to remember.

Frederick Buechner

A Room Called Remember

Pictures from Heaven

We've all grown up with different pictures of what a father is. Some of the pictures are underexposed: The image is washed out and weak, a passive father maybe, or one without passion. Others are overexposed: The image is dark and frightening, an alcoholic father maybe, or one who is just angry all the time. A few are torn pictures: Only a partial image is left, maybe because the father died or opted for a divorce or just wasn't around to complete the picture. Still others are distorted pictures: The full image is there, but some part of the image is out of balance, too much discipline and too little affection, too much talking and too little listening. In my case, there were simply too few pictures. And the few I had were not ones you'd want to pass down to your kids.

Where do you go if those are the pictures you've been left with? Where do you go to find pictures of the Father—pictures of how to choose to bless—especially if there aren't any Doug Barrams in your life to show you?

"In the beginning was the Word," John began his gospel, "and the Word was with God, and the Word was God" (1:1). After a few parenthetical remarks, John completed his thought. "And the Word became flesh, and dwelt among us, and we beheld His glory, glory as of the only begotten from the Father, full of grace and truth" (v. 14). John went on to explain: "No man has seen God at any time; the only begotten God, who is in the bosom of the

Father, He has explained Him" (v. 18). Later in John's gospel, Jesus said to the disciples in the upper room, "He who has seen Me has seen the Father" (14:9).

Another way of expressing those thoughts might be this: In the beginning we had no pictures of God, so he sent his Son to show us the pictures. The Word became flesh to make the invisible, visible. To bring what was far, near. To show us the Father. The patriarchs and prophets told us about him. Jesus showed us, a picture at a time.

Where do you go to get pictures of the Father? You go to Jesus, and you look at the pictures.

"Show, don't tell" is a key principle of writing. The point is that pictures are more impactive than words. The stronger the picture is the fewer words you need to explain it. That's why, I think, the words of Christ in the Scriptures are so few.

"Let him who is without sin cast the first stone" (see John 8:7).

"Render unto Caesar what is Caesar's, and to God what is God's" (see Matthew 22:21).

"Today you shall be with Me in Paradise" (Luke 23:43).

The pictures above those captions are so strong that few words are needed. Some of the clearest, most striking pictures Jesus blessed us with are pictures of him with people. We'll look at five of them: The woman at the well. The washing of the disciples' feet. The commission of Peter. The hemorrhaging woman. And the picture of our Heavenly Father.

THE WOMAN AT THE WELL

The picture of Jesus with the woman at the well is found in John 4.

She came to the well at noon, the hottest hour of the day, and that alone whispers something of her reputation. Most women would have come early in the morning or at dusk when it was cool. This woman had had five husbands, and she wasn't married to the man she was living with then. So she came midday to fill her jar, probably to avoid the gossip, the stares, the fingers pointed in her direction. When she met Jesus at that well and he asked for a drink, she was startled. "How is it that You, being a Jew, ask me for a drink since I am a Samaritan woman?" It struck her as odd, partly because he was a Jew and the Jews had no dealings with the Samaritans, and partly because he was a man and men had little social contact with women in the Middle East. Yet to her and to her alone, he gave one of the greatest revelations in all of Scripture, that "God is spirit, and those who worship Him must worship in spirit and truth."

The short conversation they had together at that well changed her life. It blessed her to know that someone like Jesus would talk to someone with her reputation. And if you read the account in John, you'll see it's a *real* conversation they had. Not a monologue but a dialogue. Not a sermon but genuine interaction. Jesus showing up in her world, meeting her where she was, talking with her about her life, and treating her with dignity and respect create a truly beautiful picture of the way God comes to each of us. Meeting us at the well where we are. Engaging us in conversation. Treating us with respect. Moving us closer and closer to him.

Doug Barram dropped lots of pictures like that into my life. He was an adult, yet he showed up in a high school world, meeting me on the football field or the gym, talking with me about my life, treating me with dignity and respect, moving me closer and closer to the well of living water.

One time in particular stands out in my memory. It was my senior year. He took seven of us who were in his Bible study—all seniors, each of whom he had led to Christ—and took us out to breakfast. He wanted to get us all together before we left for college. After we finished eating, he had all of us tell what our goals and dreams were. My brother Jeff said he wanted to be a doctor, which he now is. One of the other guys wanted to be a commercial pilot. One by one we told each other our dreams. When it was my turn, I said I wanted to get my doctorate, write books, and help people, and everybody at the table laughed. I was a terrible student. I got into college on academic probation and into seminary that way and into my doctoral program that way. So they had good reason to laugh. But two people at the table didn't laugh: my brother, who has always been wonderfully supportive, and Doug. He believed I could do it. He treated me with such dignity and respect. He always did but especially that day when the others at the table were kidding me. I never forgot that picture of this adult meeting with a bunch of high school kids around a table, engaging us in a dialogue about our lives, treating us all with such dignity and respect.

Just as Jesus did.

The Washing of the Disciples' Feet

The second picture is mounted in the Scriptures in John 13.

In the upper room the night of his arrest, Jesus was celebrating a last meal with his disciples. Before the meal, much to their surprise, he washed their feet. This was the duty of a servant: to greet the guests with a basin of water and a towel, take off their sandals, and wash the dirt from their feet. "I came not to be served but to serve," Jesus said earlier in his ministry (see Matthew 20:28). This is one of the pictures that shows us he meant it.

And it's a picture for all of us. To think that Jesus would do that for us. That he would serve us. Cleanse us. Refresh us. Make us feel like a guest in his presence. What a picture of blessing! Even if we've always been treated like outcasts or the uninvited or tagalongs, he sees us as honored guests. And he stoops to serve us.

I have a similar picture from my mom, who blessed me with so many Christlike pictures over my life. I have a picture of her helping me with my can collection. I had a friend who had started a beer can collection, and we decided to team up and enter the collection in the state fair. We were so excited about it. My mom helped by driving us around at night to look for cans. She'd stay out with us till twelve or one in the morning sometimes, sitting in the car so patiently, while he and I rummaged through trash cans and Dumpsters. All for a few cans? No. All for me. It was her way of serving, her way of washing my feet, her way of saying that I mattered, that what I got excited about was important. Even if it was just a collection of cans.

THE COMMISSION OF PETER

This particular picture is found in Matthew 16.

Jesus took this brash and impulsive fisherman, asked him one question, and on the basis of his answer commissioned him to lead his church. Actually it's not what Jesus heard in Peter's answer. It's what he saw in Peter's potential. Where others saw only the sharp and abrasive edges of a rock, Jesus saw a foundation. Where others saw unpredictability, Jesus saw stability. Where others saw the rough hands of a fisherman, Jesus saw hands that held the keys of the kingdom of heaven. He saw Peter not as who he was but who he was to become.

What a picture of blessing in Peter's life. What a picture of blessing for each of us when we are told that we have been predestined to be conformed to the image of Christ (Romans 8:29), that he who has begun a good work in us will bring it to completion (Philippians 1:6). What potential he sees in us.

I was blessed with a picture early in life that told me I had potential. I never forgot it. I was nine or ten, and things around the house were tight, so all of us boys helped out however we could. I threw a paper route in the morning, giving most of the money to Mom. In the afternoon I delivered doughnuts from a local bakery. They gave me a big wicker basket and filled it with fresh, hot doughnuts. I went door-to-door selling them. What I couldn't sell by the end of the day, I took to the home of the woman who played Kitty on *Gunsmoke*. I'd go to the servants' entrance, and whatever I had left, they would always buy. Well, one day I was going door-to-door through a strip shopping center, and I breezed through the door of a shoe store. Either I didn't see the "No Soliciting" sign, or I didn't know what soliciting meant—I can't remember now. But I do remember the manager going berserk when he saw me. I backed away, and he went off on a tirade, lecturing me about trespassing, not reading signs, interfering with business. "I've always thrown out every salesman who's come through that door. What are *you* selling?"

When he asked, I automatically went into the sales pitch I had memorized. "Fresh, hot doughnuts. Chocolate covered. Honey glazed. Melt in your mouth. Make you a hero to whoever you serve them to."

Then he broke into this huge smile. "I'll take a dozen."

I put them in a white sack, stapled it, and handed it to him.

"Are they really fresh?" he asked.

"Truck's right down the street," I said, smiling.

And then he told me, "Do me a favor. When you grow up, I want you to come see me and work for me. You'll be a great shoe salesman."

I smiled and thanked him and walked out. When I grew up, I didn't go back for that job, but I never forgot the offer. I never forgot the man who looked at the kid with the wicker basket, turning his scowl suddenly to a smile, buying a sackful of doughnuts, and telling me, a kid, "When you grow up, I want you to come see me and work for me. You'll be a great shoe salesman." Imagine the blessing that nine-year-old kid walked away with that day. In my memory, the picture is as clear as the day it was taken. And as dear.

THE HEMORRHAGING WOMAN

The picture is one of my favorites. You can find it framed in Luke 8.

Jesus was on his way to heal a dying twelve-year-old girl, the daughter of a synagogue official named Jairus. As he was walking, the crowds were pressing against him, so the scene was fairly intense. A girl's life was at stake. An eager crowd was packed around him. And into this scene a woman with constant bleeding pushed through the crowd, thinking to herself, *If I can just get close enough to touch his garment, that will be enough.* Finally she got close enough and touched the fringe of his garment. Barely a tug. But he felt it. And he stopped. He was sensitive to the touch because it was a touch of faith. He called to her, and she came, trembling, and fell down before him. And ever so tenderly he told her, "Daughter, your faith has made you well; go in peace."

It is one of my favorite pictures because it shows me how sensitive Jesus was to the slight touch of faith we can extend to him. We don't have to have the right words. Or the right timing. Or the right anything. All we have to do is reach out to him. And he stops for us.

It's one of my favorite pictures because it reminds me of a picture of my mom—lots of pictures of my mom actually. During my senior year in high school, Jeff and I had a ritual we went through with several of our friends. After we dropped off our Saturday night dates, if we had a date, we'd meet at Jack-in-the-Box at eleven, and together we'd wolf down an entire menu of tacos, burgers, fries, and shakes. Then about midnight, Jeff and I would head home for another ritual.

We'd walk down the hall to Mom's room, where she lay sleeping in the dark, touch her to wake her up, and then flop down on either side of her and talk about our evening—our dates, the movie we saw, the people we met. The conversation would drift to what our week had been like, what went well, what didn't. We shared our dreams, telling each other the details of our lives. Then one Saturday night, after months of this ritual, a thought struck me. "Mom?" I asked. "Does it bother you, us waking you up so late to talk?"

"Boys," she said, patting us in the dark. "I can *always* go back to sleep. But I won't always have you boys here to talk to. Wake me up anytime."

And I knew she meant it. She loved us so much that she put our needs before her own. Even after midnight when she was asleep. Even when she had to get up early the next day. She was never so tired or so pressured that she couldn't talk with her boys in the dark. She always had time. *Always.*

THE PICTURE OF OUR HEAVENLY FATHER

The picture is tucked away in Luke 15.

Jesus presented the picture to show the Pharisees the joy there is in heaven when just one wayward person turns around and comes home to the Father's arms. The story is a familiar one. The prodigal son decided he wanted to see the world and sow some wild oats along the way. But when the money from his inheritance ran out, he was destitute in a distant land, and the only job he could get was in a pigsty. What brought him to his senses and put him on the road back was a picture of his father's generosity. "How many of my father's hired men have more than enough bread, but I am dying here with hunger!" As the son made his way home, his father spotted him. Look at the picture of how he responded.

While he was still a long way off, his father saw him, and felt compassion for him, and ran and embraced him, and kissed him. And the son said to him, "Father, I have sinned against heaven and in your sight; I am no longer worthy to be called your son."

But the father said to his slaves, "Quickly bring out the best robe and put it on him, and put a ring on his hand and sandals on his feet; and bring the fattened calf, kill it, and let us eat and be merry; for this son of mine was dead, and has come to life again; he was lost, and has been found. And they began to be merry." (vv. 20-24)

It's all there in a picture. The eyes that searched for him. The heart that went out to him. The legs that ran to him. The arms that embraced him. The lips that kissed him. It's all there. And it's for all for us. It's even for all of us who never received a blessing from our fathers, who never received the attention, the understanding, the compassion, the embraces, the forgiveness, the restoration, the love, the joy, or the delight of a father in his son.

Someone once said that a child is not likely to find a father in God unless he finds something of God in his father. I never found something of God in my biological father. But I did find it in my spiritual father, Doug Barram. And finding something of God in that father made it easier to find a father in God. The first Bible verse Doug gave me to memorize was Hebrews 13:5. I memorized it from the Phillips translation. "God has said: I will in no wise fail thee, neither will I in any wise forsake thee." I'll never forget that verse and the impact it first had on me. God said he *would not* fail me, *would not* forsake me. He wouldn't one day pack up his bags and walk out of my life. Under *any* circumstances. He was going to stay. And he was going to stay *forever*.

Could there be a father like that in all the universe?

Jesus said there was, and he took this picture out of his wallet to show us what he looks like.

Is it any wonder that those of us who are serious about living a life of blessing should look at the life of Christ to be our guide? In just five pictures we can see so much! (And we could look at a hundred more pictures!)

With the woman at the well, we see how he blessed a near outcast with dignity and respect. How he modeled honesty and a hopeful future for someone who needed it so much—like the people we sit next to every day.

As he washed the disciples' feet, Jesus showed us how humble people who serve and honor others leave an unforgettable picture of blessing in others' lives. Something each of us can and should do.

In the commissioning of Peter, Jesus looked past flaws and imperfections and saw Peter not for who he was but who he would become. How powerfully we bless others when we don't write them off with "They'll never change!"—and instead realize how he can change us as well as them.

With a hemorrhaging woman, Jesus showed amazing sensitivity in noticing the smallest touch. He showed us how we need to see those who are timidly reaching—not shouting—for our attention . . . people, even family members, who need our touch and blessing so much.

With the story of the prodigal son, Jesus illustrated a father's blessing without shame when there's repentance. Without conditions when there's conviction. Without cutting words when a child comes home, crying tears of remorse.

If you want to see a picture of the Father, look at Jesus.

If you want to see a picture of how to bless, look at Jesus.

And especially look at that horrible, beautiful picture Jesus gave us of blessing others as he hung on a cross.

I do not remember much of what happened just before or after the stunning announcement, but an image of the moment when I first learned the news has remained fixed in my mind for over thirty years. For many of us, the memory of that November afternoon in 1963 feels as though it has been frozen forever in photographic form, unaffected by the ravages of time that erode and degrade most other memories.

Daniel L. Schacter, speaking about the assassination of President Kennedy

Searching for Memory

The Horrible, Beautiful Picture

I f you had lived during the Civil War period in American history, you would have remembered vividly where you were, who you were with, and what you were doing the moment you heard that President Lincoln had been assassinated. The same is true if you were alive a century later when President Kennedy was assassinated. Psychologists term this phenomenon a "'flashbulb memory,' a memory that is made especially crisp and clear because of its emotional implications."[1] The closer you were to the deceased, the more vivid the picture burned into your mind. Imagine then, with Peter being one of the three disciples closest to Christ, the vividness of the picture he carried with him the rest of his life.

I'm not talking about the picture of his denial. I'm talking about a memory filled with even more emotion than that one. Although John was the only disciple to stand at the foot of the cross and watch the entire Crucifixion, it is likely that Peter saw at least a glimpse of it from a distance. I say this on the basis of a verse from his epistle. Giving us advice on how to endure unjust suffering, Peter pointed to Jesus dying on the cross as our example: "While being reviled, He did not revile in return; while suffering, He uttered no threats, but kept entrusting Himself to Him who judges righteously" (1 Peter 2:23). The verse suggests Peter witnessed at least some of the mocking and the suffering, along with the very moment of Christ's death. The last part of the verse is reminiscent of Christ's last words, "Father, into thy hands I commend My spirit" (Luke 23:46, KJV).

How close Peter stood, how long he watched, how much he saw—we don't know. But here is something of the picture that burned in his memory.

By the time Jesus reached the hill outside Jerusalem's walls, he was a horrible sight. He had been up all night, pushed from one interrogation to another. Already he had been beaten in a brutal game the soldiers played, a mocking crown of thorns mashed onto his head, puncturing his scalp to form seeping wells of blood. His face throbbed, the bruises on it darkening as they swelled. The flesh on his back, arms, and chest had been eaten by a cat-o'-nine-tails, the merciless whip that had laid bare the pink of his muscles and the white of his bone. Jesus had just come from being paraded through the narrow streets of the city where he had staggered under the weight of the crossbeam he shouldered, time and again stumbling from exhaustion.

A grotesque parade had brought him here, outside the city walls where the dirty work of the empire was done. The place was called Calvary, a stoic, stone hill sloping down from the eastern end of the city, staring out over the Kidron Valley. Jesus stood on that hill with two other men slated for execution: Hardened and hateful, they were career criminals.

The crowd gathered early that morning. Gawkers, hecklers, and religious representatives came to make sure the job got done, that there were no escapes, no rescues. Soldiers stripped the three men. One by one they stretched them out over the splintery wood, while several of the soldiers sat on each prisoner so the spiker could do his work without the prisoner twisting free. The criminals went first, cursing and swearing as they were strong-armed into submission and writhed on the wood.

They came for Jesus next. He submitted to the soldiers, then to the nails. One was pounded into each arm, right below the wrist at the heel of the palm. His legs were twisted sideways, pushed toward his pelvis, and one foot was placed over the other for a final nail. The clank of metal against metal echoed off the stone walls.

The bases of the crosses were aligned so they would slide into place as they were lifted. Ropes were draped around the crossbeam and the slack cinched out of them, awaiting the heave of the soldiers who had spaced themselves evenly on either side of the cruel mast. Jesus' cross was raised, jostled into position, and thudded into postholes in the stone, tearing flesh and rasping bone. The pain pulled air into his lungs and held it there with a tight-fisted grip.

"FATHER, FORGIVE THEM"

Slowly the grip eased, allowing Jesus just enough strength to push himself up from the nail in his feet. He drew a breath and exhaled a prayer.

"Father, forgive them; for they do not know what they are doing."

The soldiers beneath the cross, who were gambling for his clothes, looked up. Over the years they had heard a lot of things from those crosses. Screaming. Cursing. Delirious rantings. Convulsive sobbings. Confessions. Challenges. They thought they'd heard everything. But they'd never heard anything like this. No one had ever extended forgiveness to his enemies. The winning soldier took the garment, and the circle around the cross dispersed.

With the soldiers gone, the consciousless crowd converged. The men around the cross crept forward, their sneering lips baring toothy smiles. They darted at Jesus like hyenas, tearing at the still-living body of a downed animal.

"Ha! You who were going to destroy the temple and rebuild it in three days, save Yourself, and come down from the cross!"

The challenge drew the crowd's laughter. When it subsided, a waiting silence followed, leaving the crowd wondering how this king of the hill would respond. He didn't. Ripples of contempt for his silence ran through the ranks of the more religious.

"He saved others; let Him save Himself if this is the Christ of God, His Chosen."

"Let this Christ, the King of Israel, now come down from the cross, so that we may see and believe!"

One of them quoted Scripture. "He trusts in God; let Him deliver Him now, if He takes pleasure in Him, for he said, 'I am the Son of God.'"

A handful of soldiers then took their turn. Each with his own spear of ridicule. A cutting remark. A jab of sarcasm. A crass comment about his nakedness. Racial slurs. Raucous laughter. They offered Jesus sour wine and some advice, "If you are the King of the Jews, save Yourself!"

The morning sun was in Jesus' face, drying the blood, as flies crowded the banks of open wounds. After the soldiers were finished with their fun, the criminals on either side of Jesus joined in, hurling their own insults. Soldiers, commoners, scribes, priests, elders, criminals—they all wanted a taste of the kill. Dogs from the garbage dumps had scrabbled up the hill, panting along the fringes of the crowd, skittishly waiting their turn.

Jesus' mother was hearing it all, watching it all, bearing it all. John stood by her side, giving her his shoulder, his tenderness, his support. Jesus looked down to them and seeing them holding each other, spoke.

"Woman, behold your son."

"Behold, your mother."

With those words Jesus entrusted the care of the mother he loved to the disciple he loved.

The sun was now high in the sky, and the fight in the criminals had been sweated out of them. They had resigned themselves to their fate. A fate they deserved. They had cursed people's lives at so many different times and in so many different ways. But when they cursed Rome by breaking its laws, Rome cursed back. The vengeance of the empire was swift, certain, and without mercy.

"TODAY, YOU WILL BE WITH ME"

From the fever in his wounds, one of the criminals drew enough fire to say one last hateful thing. "Are You not the Christ? Save Yourself and us!"

Jesus hung there, silently, wearily, his pendulous weight straining at the nails. Though he didn't defend himself, the other criminal defended him. "Do you not even fear God, since you are under the same sentence of condemnation? And we indeed justly, for we are receiving what we deserve for our deeds; but this man has done nothing wrong."

For the past three hours the man defending Jesus had been watching the evil, the hate, and the insults that had been thrown at him. Three hours of people cursing him, and never once did Jesus curse back. Never once did he argue. Never once did he accuse. Never once did he show any animosity at all. The only words he returned were ones of forgiveness—genuinely, humbly, and tenderly spoken.

The man looked at Jesus, glancing first at the caption Pilate had placed over his head: "JESUS THE NAZARENE, KING OF THE JEWS." Then he looked at the picture. In it he saw a love he had never known existed.

"Jesus." His words were timid from their unworthiness, and there was shame in them for the words that came cursing from his mouth earlier. "Remember me when You come into Your kingdom."

Through lips that were parched and split, Jesus answered him. "Truly I say to you, today you will be with Me in Paradise."

Forgiveness. Love. Mercy.

It's all there in that picture.

A picture of someone giving a blessing to relationships that offered only curses.

A picture of someone giving light to relationships that huddled in the darkness.

A picture of someone giving life to a relationship that was dead.

It's all there. In that horrible, beautiful picture.

Sometimes the briefest moments capture us, force us to take them in, and demand that we live the rest of our lives in reference to them.

Lucy Grealy

Autobiography of a Face

FOURTEEN

The Light Shining

The moments of Christ's execution that Peter witnessed forced him to take them in, demanding he live the rest of his life in reference to them. How could you see a picture like that and it *not* change you? How could you walk away without those images going with you, living within you, burning within you?

Peter did live the rest of his life in reference to that picture, and his writings reflect it. A dominant theme in his epistles is how we as Christians should face suffering, particularly suffering we don't deserve. As his example, he shows us a picture. He shows us Jesus on the cross. He takes the Savior's response to his suffering and applies it to three significant relationships where we might encounter some measure of suffering too. The first is our relationship as citizens. The second is our relationship as workers. The third is our relationship as spouses. The circles of relationships are concentric, each tighter and more intimate than the one before.

If you open your Bibles to the context of 1 Peter 2:13–3:9, you'll see that the picture of the cross is central. Preceding it are the applications to our relationship with the government and our relationship with our work. Following the picture of the cross is the application to our relationship with our spouse. Verse 21 of chapter 2 ties the picture into the preceding relationships. "For you have been called for this purpose, since Christ also suffered for you, leaving you an example for you to follow in His steps." Verse 1 of chapter 3 ties the picture to the following relationship. *"In the same way,* you wives . . ."

With that context in mind, let's look at the text, starting first with the example of Christ on the cross.

THE LIGHT OF THE WORLD SHINING FROM CALVARY

> For you have been called for this purpose, since Christ also suffered for you, leaving you an example for you to follow in His steps, "who committed no sin, nor was any deceit found in His mouth;" and while being reviled, He did not revile in return; while suffering, He uttered no threats, but kept entrusting Himself to Him who judges righteously; and He Himself bore our sins in His body on the cross, that we might die to sin and live to righteousness; for by His wounds you were healed. For you were continually straying like sheep, but now you have returned to the Shepherd and Guardian of your souls. (1 Peter 2:21-25)

The picture is an answer to the question: How do you respond to the darkness when it encroaches on these three primary relationships?

The answer? You shine a light.

In his book *Telling the Truth: The Gospel as Tragedy, Comedy and Fairy Tale,* Frederick Buechner says that the gospel is the "tale of a light breaking into the world that even the darkness cannot overcome."[1] That light has the power to change our relationships.

But not all relationships respond to light, however much we give. The reality is, some people prefer the darkness. Some people couldn't care less if we've been hurt or offended or unjustly treated. To show us how to respond to such people, Peter pointed to the cross. His advice in such relationships? Entrust ourselves to him who judges righteously. Leave the avenging to God. It is an act of faith, perhaps the supreme act of faith. By not demanding our day in court, we're saying, in effect, that we believe there is a just God who rules the universe and that one day he will deal decisively with the injustice. If we believe that, *really* believe that, we will entrust our case to him instead of taking matters into our own hands. The problem with taking matters into our own hands is that in the process justice often slips through our fingers. And what we are left holding is a grudge, which plots revenge.

"The problem with revenge," notes Lewis Smedes, "is that it never gets what it wants; it never evens the score. Fairness never comes. The chain reaction set off by every act of vengeance always takes its unhindered course. It ties both the injured and the injurer to an escalator of pain. Both are stuck on the escalator as long as parity is demanded, and the escalator never stops, never lets anyone off."[2]

Here again, forgiveness is key. Ideally, forgiveness brings reconciliation in relationships. But not always. It takes two to be reconciled. Don't let your forgiveness be predicated on another person's response. We forgive because it is the right thing to do, because it is what we are commanded to do, and because it is what Christ would do.

Peter takes the light shining from the cross and focuses it on our relationships. In each relationship our role is different, but our responsibility is the same. Speaking of those roles, Gerald Sittser stresses the importance of choice:

> We do not always have the freedom to choose the roles we must play in life, but we can choose how we are going to play the roles we are given. . . . We can return evil for evil, or we can overcome evil with good. It is this power to choose that adds dignity to our humanity and gives us the ability to transcend our circumstances, thus releasing us from living as mere victims.[3]

The first relationship Peter focuses on is our relationship to governmental authority.

BRINGING LIGHT AND LIFE TO OUR
GOVERNMENTAL RELATIONSHIPS

> Submit yourselves for the Lord's sake to every human institution,
> whether to a king as the one in authority, or to governors as sent
> by him for the punishment of evildoers and the praise of those who
> do right. For such is the will of God that by doing right you may
> silence the ignorance of foolish men. Act as free men, and do not
> use your freedom as a covering for evil, but use it as bondslaves of
> God. Honor all men; love the brotherhood, fear God, honor the
> king. (1 Peter 2:13-17)

At the time Peter wrote this, Nero was the king he was telling his readers
to honor. He was a corrupt and wicked king who was responsible for the per-
secution that led to Peter's own crucifixion. But even under the darkest
regimes, light can still shine from our lives. Sometimes it has a transforming
effect—"by doing right you may silence the ignorance of foolish men" (2:15).
But that is not why we do it. We do it because it is "the will of God" (v. 15),
not for the outcome it may produce.

Forgiveness is a choice. And we are always free to make it, even in the
most insufferable circumstances, like the circumstances Victor Frankl and so
many Jews experienced in World War II.

> We who lived in concentration camps can remember the men who
> walked through the huts comforting others, giving away their last
> piece of bread. They may have been few in number, but they offer
> sufficient proof that everything can be taken from a man but one
> thing: the last of the human freedoms—to choose one's attitude in
> any given set of circumstances, to choose one's own way.[4]

Peter next shone the light of the cross on a second relationship.

BRINGING LIGHT AND LIFE TO OUR WORKING RELATIONSHIPS

> Servants, be submissive to your masters with all respect, not only
> to those who are good and gentle, but also to those who are
> unreasonable. For this finds favor, if for the sake of conscience
> toward God a man bears up under sorrows when suffering unjustly.
> For what credit is there if, when you sin and are harshly treated,
> you endure it with patience? But if when you do what is right and
> suffer for it you patiently endure it, this finds favor with God.
> (1 Peter 2:18-20)

The economy in our country today is different than the one in the Roman empire. Still, the principle has application. Most of us at some time or another have had employers or supervisors who were unreasonable or who treated us harshly for something we didn't deserve. What is the response that finds favor with God? To patiently endure it.

Again, it's a choice. The same choice Martin Luther King Jr. made when he was subjected to all kinds of abuse as a black man campaigning for civil rights. "As my sufferings mounted I soon realized that there were two ways in which I could respond to my situation—either to react with bitterness or seek to transform the suffering into a creative force."[5]

Peter then turned his attention to the marriage relationship.

BRINGING LIGHT AND LIFE TO OUR MARRIAGE RELATIONSHIPS

> In the same way, you wives, be submissive to your own husbands
> so that even if any of them are disobedient to the word, they may
> be won without a word by the behavior of their wives, as they
> observe your chaste and respectful behavior. And let not your
> adornment be merely external—braiding the hair, and wearing gold
> jewelry, or putting on dresses; but let it be the hidden person of the

heart, with the imperishable quality of a gentle and quiet spirit, which is precious in the sight of God. For in this way in former times the holy women also, who hoped in God, used to adorn themselves, being submissive to their own husbands. Thus Sarah obeyed Abraham, calling him lord, and you have become her children if you do what is right without being frightened by any fear.

You husbands likewise, live with your wives in an understanding way, as with a weaker vessel, since she is a woman; and grant her honor as a fellow heir of the grace of life, so that your prayers may not be hindered. (1 Peter 3:1-7)

Notice how the woman with the unbelieving husband is asked to respond: with pictures, not words. Pictures of a life transformed by God. Pictures that reveal the hidden person of the heart. Pictures that are precious in God's sight, regardless how her mate views them.

When I think of pictures of a woman with chaste and respectful behavior, I think of my mom. Although she wasn't a Christian until later in life, she was always a very moral person. She didn't drink, didn't swear, didn't even yell. Her adornment was truly the hidden person of the heart. My mother wore that gentle and quiet spirit so beautifully. Her husband was the kind of man Peter refers to, one who was disobedient to the Word. Unfortunately he wasn't around to see the lovely pictures develop in her life. Fortunately my brothers and I were.

Peter next shifted from specifics to generalizations, giving universal principles for every relationship.

BRINGING LIGHT AND LIFE TO EVERY RELATIONSHIP

To sum up, let all be harmonious, sympathetic, brotherly, kindhearted, and humble in spirit; not returning evil for evil, or insult for insult, but giving a blessing instead; for you were called

112

for the very purpose that you might inherit a blessing.
(1 Peter 3:8–9)

The hope of living out the blessing is that it will transform our relationships. But even if some relationships aren't transformed, we will still benefit, as Lewis Smedes notes: "The climax of forgiveness takes two, I know. But you can have the reality of forgiving without its climax. You do not always need a thing whole to enjoy it all. A blossom has real beauty even if it never becomes a flower. A climb can be successful though we do not reach the summit. Forgiving is real even if it stops at the healing of the forgiver."[6]

What do we do when the government is insufferable, when the employer is unreasonable, when the mate is unresponsive? We don't respond in kind. We respond in kindness. That is the way Christ responded. And that is what finds favor with God. As Martin Luther King Jr. noted so well: "Returning hate for hate multiplies hate, adding deeper darkness to a night already devoid of stars. Darkness cannot drive out darkness; only light can do that. Hate cannot drive out hate; only love can do that."[7]

"I am the light of the world," Jesus said (John 8:12). In the Sermon on the Mount, he said that we, too, are the light of the world (Matthew 5:14).

Together we can shine.

And together we can drive out the darkness.

That is the good news of the gospel. That light *can* drive out darkness. That love *can* conquer hate. It seems too good to be true. It seems almost like a fairy tale that no grownup would ever consider taking seriously. Maybe that is why Jesus says that unless we humble ourselves like little children, we will never enter the kingdom of heaven.

"When I was ten," C. S. Lewis said, "I read fairy tales in secret and would have been ashamed if I had been found doing so. Now that I am fifty, I read them openly. When I became a man, I put away childish things, including the fear of childishness and the desire to be very grown up."[8]

I'd like to share with you one of my favorite fairy tales: *Sleeping Beauty.* The literary versions are by Charles Perrault and the Brothers Grimm, but it is the film version I want to focus on. At the celebration of the birth of the royal princess, three good fairies—Flora, Fauna, and Meriwether—come to dote over her and to bestow their blessings. Before they do, one of them announces:

Each of us
the child may bless
with a single gift,
no more, no less.

One blesses the princess with the gift of beauty. One with the gift of song. But as the other fairy starts to give her blessing, the sinister-looking witch, Malificent, storms into the room. "I, too, shall bestow a gift on the sweet princess. Listen well, all of you. The princess shall indeed grow in grace and beauty, beloved by all. But before the sun sets on her sixteenth birthday, she shall prick her finger on the spindle of a spinning wheel and die."

Everyone cringes at the curse. But suddenly one of the good fairies remembers. "Don't despair. Meriwether still has her gift."

"Then can she undo it?" asks one of the fairies.

"No," says the other fairy. "Malificent's powers are too great. But she can help."

Then Meriwether steps forward with her blessing:

Sweet princess, if through this wicked witch's trick,
a spindle should your finger prick,
a ray of hope there still may be,
in the gift I give to thee.
Not in death but in sleep,
the fateful prophecy will keep,
and from this slumber you shall awake,
when true love's kiss the spell shall break.

The scene ends with the hopeful chorus, "True love conquers all."[9]

At the end of the fairy tale, true love does conquer all.

It conquers all in the Good Friday tale too. For when the Prince of Peace comes to our part of the forest and sees us lying there under the curse of

114

death, he kneels by our side and kisses us. The kiss breaks the curse. And the beautiful blessings that have been sleeping in us all for so long . . . awaken.

He is our Prince. That is his picture. And of all the pictures he left behind, that is the one that blesses us most.

In the studio where I work, there is a wash basin. Above the wash basin is a mirror. I stop at this place several times each day to tidy up and look at myself in the mirror. Alongside the mirror is the photograph of a troublesome woman.

Robert Fulghum

All I Really Need to Know I Learned in Kindergarten

To Get the Message

The "troublesome woman" in the photograph on Robert Fulghum's mirror is Mother Teresa. The occasion of the photograph was her acceptance of the Nobel Peace Prize in Oslo, Norway.

"Each time I look in the mirror at myself," writes Fulghum, "I also look at her face. In it I have seen more than I can tell; and from what I see, I understand more than I can say."[1]

That is the power of a picture. It speaks to us. It speaks to the core of who we are. Often it communicates more than we can express, speaking to us in a language too deep for words.

"I do not speak her language," Fulghum said. "Yet the eloquence of her life speaks to me. And I am chastised and blessed at the same time. I do not believe one person can do much in the world. Yet there she stood, in Oslo, affecting the world around. I do not believe in her version of God. But the power of her faith shames me."[2]

We've looked at pictures of Christ that can bless us. Now let's look at the lives of two extraordinary people who can teach us about the blessing as well.

During one sad and tragic week in September of 1997, pictures of that face on Fulghum's mirror were set beside pictures of the face of Princess Diana.

Life's special tribute to Diana juxtaposes a number of their photos, from those in their childhood to those at their funerals. The magazine introduced the pairing of photographs with these words: "Life seldom linked Mother Teresa, eighty-seven, and Princess Diana, thirty-six, despite a much-reproduced photograph of their last meeting, earlier this year. But an accident of timing links them in death. Rarely had the founder of the Missionaries of Charity seemed so much a celebrity, or the Princess of Wales so saintly. Comparisons that would otherwise never have occurred suddenly felt inevitable."[3]

So did the contrasts.

The two women couldn't have been more different. One was a companion to the richest of the rich. The other, to the poorest of the poor. One had bills last year for personal grooming that totaled $240,000, a tenth of which went for manicures alone.[4] The other was living out the vow of poverty she had taken seventy years earlier. One life was lived in the photoflash of celebrity. The other, among the shadows of death.

In the photographic tribute to Diana mentioned earlier, one picture brings the two women together. It's the one where Diana and Mother Teresa are standing next to each other outside a New York City Missionaries of Charity residence. In the picture the contrast between the princess and the pauper is striking.

The princess is tall and stately. The pauper, stooped-shouldered and short. The princess is wearing a crisp white suit. The pauper, a wrinkled sari. The head of the princess is crowned with golden hair. The head of the pauper is covered. The princess is wearing expensive heels. The pauper, sandals.

The two had come together for the first time five years earlier. Mother Teresa had invited Diana to Calcutta. In 1992 the princess went. But not to Calcutta, not at first. First she went to Rome, where the ailing nun was hospitalized. They met several times in the years that followed, and finally Diana did go to Calcutta, where she dispensed medicine to the sick, along with sweets.

Who knows how the pictures of that pauper affected the princess? We know they led her to the pauper's bedside. They also led her to the conclusion that she was the subject in the relationship, not the sovereign, for from the moment of their first meeting, Princess Diana considered Mother Teresa her mentor.

How different, though, was the mentor from her student. "Mother Teresa was a saint built on the old model, pious, chaste, ascetic, prayerful, poor," said one reporter. "Princess Diana, the only other contender for media sainthood, was none of those things."[5]

How Very Different They Were . . .

Princess Di was the most photographed woman in the world. And among the most photogenic. After her death the market was flooded with Diana photographs, Diana magazines, Diana books.

One group of photographs in particular grabbed my attention. They are in a book with a white background and a black-and-white photo of Princess Di centered on the cover.[6] Inside, the pictures are arranged chronologically. They begin with a barefoot Diana on a blanket on her first birthday. They end with a coffin at Westminster Abbey. In between are the pictures that tell the story of her life. A lot of them are closeups. Most of them could have made the cover of any fashion magazine in the world. All of them are beautiful.

But I doubt they are the ones *she* would have chosen, not if she could choose them now. Now that she's gone, I think she would rather not be remembered for how photogenic she was, how stunning she looked in designer hats, or how exquisitely she graced the restaurants of the French Riviera. I think she would want to be remembered by other pictures, pictures that revealed other things about her, pictures that would leave behind positive messages in the lives of those she loved. Pictures that would bless the lives of her sons.

Diana left behind a lot of pictures of her and her two boys, William, the future king of England, and Harry, the younger prince. Her apartment in Kensington Palace was almost a shrine to her love for them, with framed photos of the boys on every wall.

In one picture her arms are wrapped around young Harry as William stands behind her, wrapping his arms around her. In another the boys are younger, propped on a piano bench, pounding away at the keys, with Diana standing behind them, smiling. In one she is with them the first day of school, they in their uniforms, she on the steps beside them. It seems like any other first-day-of-school photograph. Except boys in royal families don't go to school. School comes to them. In the form of private lessons, personal tutors. But Diana thought an important part of their education was to learn what life was like outside the palace walls, so she broke a time-honored tradition and sent the boys to school.

Princess Di left behind lots of other pictures with her boys.

In one she is being buried by her eager younger son with shovels of sand on a beach, accompanied by a bunch of his friends. In another she is posed with a laughing William on one side of her, his arm resting on her shoulder. On the other side, a more subdued Harry is leaning into her, comfortable and relaxed. In yet another picture the three of them ride up a chairlift in Colorado. And then there is the picture where the camera freezes them at the end of a log ride at Disney World in Florida, the three of them wet and wild and wonderfully happy, scrunched together in the log.

What a memory for two boys who now have nothing *but* memories of their mother.

Diana was forthright about her failures, but motherhood wasn't one of them. The thing in her life she felt most proud of was being a mom. When the boys came home from school, she dropped everything. Everything else, every*one* else had to wait. Even heads of state. "I want to bring them up with security," Diana once said. "I hug my children to death and get in bed with them at night. I always feed them love and affection; it's so important."[7]

"When she was with her boys," one reporter commented, "her delight was not only palpable but irresistible. Of all the images of Diana that have burned into the public memory, few are more incandescent than one from Toronto six years ago. As Harry and William approach, their mother rushes to meet them, her body canted forward, her arms flung wide, with a smile that would light the darkest heart."[8]

Of all the pictures she left behind, I think that is the one she would most want remembered. The one with the arms that say "I've missed you so much." With the eyes that sparkle and the smile that says a thousand "I love yous."

What greater picture of blessing could a mother give to her children? A picture that says, "You are the delight of my life." A picture that brings life and light.

YET VERY MUCH THE SAME

How very different Diana and Mother Teresa were . . . yet how very much the same.

In *US News & World Report,* Michael Satchell noted the similarities with eloquence: "In an age of celebrity worship, there were common points in the lives of the tiny, wizened woman and the willowy, beautiful princess, even as their deaths drew a poignant and ironic counterpoint. Adored by millions, the tragic, privileged Diana was sanctified as much for her beauty and fame as for her willingness to reject the stiff traditions of British royalty and openly embrace the sick and handicapped. Mother Teresa, whose Missionaries of Charity minister to millions of people worldwide, was revered as a 'living saint' whose lifetime of caring for the destitute and the dying earned her the Nobel Peace Prize in 1979.

"The two women shared a compassion for the less fortunate and a deep love for children. Their final meeting took place last June at the Missionaries of Charity convent in the Bronx. The ailing missionary stepped out of her wheelchair to stroll with Diana. Arm in arm, the pair kissed, hugged, and prayed in a scene the British press dubbed as the most remarkable royal walk-about ever."[9]

Princess Diana *was* different from the royals that came before. She didn't stand detached from the crowds, waving a gloved hand as she passed. She stopped, reached into the crowds, and touched people. In 1987, when London opened its first medical unit dedicated exclusively to AIDS patients, she shook hands with a young man infected with the virus. It was a simple gesture of human kindness, but it spoke volumes to a world that shunned lepers. "With a handshake, she educated the world about compassion, love and understanding," said David Harvey, director of the National Policy Center for Children, Youth and Families in Washington.[10]

The education she offered didn't come from a textbook or a lecture or even from a word.

It came from a picture.

The princess left behind still other pictures, pictures that brought life and light to others. One of them shows her reaching down to touch a handicapped Kuwati girl, who is looking up with her buckteeth smile at the perfectly straight teeth of a princess, who is smiling back with such proud-to-meet-you genuineness.[11]

Another picture shows the princess ladling out stew for African children.[12]

Yet another shows her holding a bouquet of flowers to the nose of a white-haired woman at a Washington home for the elderly.[13]

She would frequently go to hospitals in the middle of the night, we are told, often alone, to offer a wordless hug, a quiet kiss, or a touch, and to see who else couldn't sleep at two in the morning.

I was touched by those pictures of compassion, as I have also been touched by the compassion in the pictures of Mother Teresa. One in particular stands out, from the cover of a photo album I came across.[14] The picture is black-and-white, but it is filtered through a shade of blue you see in shadows at dusk. Her characteristic white sari with its striped hem covers her head. Her eyes are closing as she holds a young girl in her arms, and her face looks tired. For fifty years she has picked up children like this off the streets. For fifty years she has held them in her arms. And for fifty years she has carried them to shelter. Her face *should* look tired.

That is the beauty of the face, a worn-down kind of beauty from so many years of searching the streets for children to hold in her arms. So much is there for us to see, as Malcolm Muggeridge noted, "In the face of a Mother Teresa I trace the very geography of Jesus' kingdom; all the contours and valleys and waterways."[15]

The pictures we leave behind. They say so much.

Surely the pictures Mother Teresa left behind influenced the pictures left behind by Diana. Through the pictures of both we have all been blessed.

Who knows how the pictures will live on in us? Who knows how they will speak, what they will say, or when they will say it? "All happenings, great and small, are parables whereby God speaks," said Malcolm Muggeridge. "The art of life is to get the message."

If that is true, what is the message of that fateful week when these pictures came together? What are the pictures saying to you and me who are struggling to raise our families, to live meaningful lives, to make a dent of a difference somewhere, somehow? Maybe the message is this, or something like this:

Look at the pictures.

First, the pictures of a princess, who is beautiful.

Then, the pictures of a pauper, who also is beautiful.

See the comparisons. See the contrasts. But most of all, see Jesus.

For all that is beautiful in this world comes from him.

You think of childhood and your thoughts stumble on a thousand pictures of your mother's hands.

The hands that untied the knotted shoestrings, buttoned the winter coat, tweaked the ear, wrote the notes when you were out of school those times. . . .

And later the hands ironed the white shirt the night of the big date, found the cuff links that were always lost, straightened the tie. . . .

As I look back through the years, her hands are what I remember most. . . .

Robert Cormier, "My Mother's Hands"

I Have Words to Spend: Reflections of a Small-Town Editor

Compensating Grace

B eing only two months old when my father left, I didn't hear the shocked sound of my mother's voice when she picked up the phone and he told her he was moving out. I didn't hear her cry. I didn't understand the despair she felt as a suddenly single parent with no job, no college degree, no money, no help from her family or the government.

In 1952 the divorce rate was four couples per thousand. No, that's not a typo. Per thousand. Suddenly she was not only in a minority but a minority that was looked down upon by the vast majority of society. She went to business school and became a career woman in the early '50s, a pioneer by circumstances not by choice. She was the thirteenth employee at First Federal Savings and Loan and ascended to the level of first vice-president. Because of her accomplishment of opening thirteen branches in 1956, the *Wall Street Journal* did a story on her.

But despite her accomplishments, her career was always secondary to her sons.

While she was solely responsible for supporting us, she was also getting us involved in sports, taking us camping, putting up posters of sports heroes on our walls, taking us to see the Dodgers when they came to Phoenix for spring training, giving us a chance to see some of the heroes in our lives such as Sandy Koufax and Don Drysdale.

She was an incredible woman.

When I show the pictures she left behind, you'll see why.

PICTURES OF MY MOTHER

Like Robert Cormier, when I think of my childhood, my thoughts stumble upon a thousand pictures of my mother's hands. But for different reasons.

She couldn't untie knotted shoestrings, button winter coats, iron shirts, or straighten ties. Simple things, but she couldn't do them. From my earliest memory, my mother's hands were bent and twisted with rheumatoid arthritis. The world wouldn't think them beautiful, but they were beautiful to me and to my brothers. They became, over the years, a symbol of her love for us.

Because of the pain in those twisted joints, my mother could not grab your hand. She never took your hand and shook it. When she took it, she touched it gently, squeezing just a part of it. Holding on to you softly. Then releasing you from her touch.

That's how she held on to each of us boys. Tenderly. Softly. With great affection and warmth. And yet loosely.

I remember when Jeff and I turned ten, she dressed us up in our finest sports coats and clip-on ties. Her hands weren't strong enough to tie a real knot, and there was no man around the house to do it. She took us to a fancy restaurant, and at dinner she made sure we knew that we were now "young men" and were expected to act as such. After dinner, she gave us each a dollar and told us, to our amazement, that we were to leave it as a tip. It was a rite-of-passage for us, for from that day on we were expected to take more and more responsibility. My mother never paid another bill or left another tip when we were with her. She would slide us the money under the table, and we would assume that duty. We were learning, through her soft hands and gentle proddings, to become gentlemen. We were beginning to grow up. And she was beginning to let go.

Mom consistently loved us passionately and yet held on to us loosely in love. The day Jeff and I turned sixteen she drove us to get our driver's licenses. Thirty minutes later she let us drive our old Volkswagen twelve hundred miles from Phoenix to Indianapolis to see our uncle. She wanted to go with us, but her hands and knees were too painful to sit scrunched in a small car for that long. Every time I look back, I marvel at the loose hold she had on our lives.

She held everything loosely. Cups. Silverware. Pencils. She even held the days loosely, never knowing whether it would be a good day or a bad one, taking what came, and taking it with grace. If her gentle touch helped us to grow up, it also provided a strong incentive to do what was right. Because her hands hurt so much, my mother was never able to spank us, but beneath her tender ways there was an underlying firmness. Worse than a spanking was when she would place her hand on ours, always gently, and speak to us, always gently, of her concern about our behavior. When she looked up at you and held your hand, you might as well have been in the grip of a lumberjack. You couldn't pull away. It would hurt her hands if you did. So you sat there. And you listened. And little by little, the warmth of her heart melted yours.

I have pictures in my mind of her typing, bending down to the keyboard, leaning a little to the right and typing at an angle. It's the way most people with rheumatoid arthritis have to type, if they can type at all. She would sit at that typewriter until the wee hours of the morning typing reports for us. I never thought much about those pictures then. Now I can't get them out of my mind . . . or my heart.

Beginning when I was seven and continuing through high school, I would often hear Mom crying in her bedroom. It was always late at night. I would climb out of bed, walk down the dark hallway, and peek into her room. One night she might have rolled over in her sleep on her deteriorating elbow and cried out in excruciating pain. Another night her medicine might have worn off, leaving her hands and knees throbbing with pain. Many times she'd go right to sleep as I watched her, wishing I could take away the pain, wondering why God didn't. Sometimes she'd see me standing in the doorway, and she'd smile and wave me in for a "late night cracker" as she called it. She kept the crackers by her bedside because the arthritis medicine upset her stomach. The crackers helped to settle it. With great effort she would unscrew the lid to the jar that held them, gently lift a cracker, and hand it to me. When we finished our crackers, I would go back to bed, and she would try to go back to sleep. But no matter how little the sleep or how great the pain the night before, she always went to work the next day. I remember that.

Because of her arthritis, Mom could only hold her granddaughters just long enough for me to take their picture together. But she talked with them and asked them questions and listened with great patience. All the while, leaving behind priceless pictures in the lives of Kari and Laura.

After I graduated from seminary, I moved home, and it was there I discovered a picture of my mom that for years had been tucked away. I was helping her with her finances, going through her records, writing checks, organizing her bills, things like that, when I pulled out a booklet of payment coupons. It was a mortgage. I looked at the address on the coupon book. It wasn't ours.

"What's this?" I asked.

She answered simply, "Pauline's place."

Pauline had been our maid throughout our growing-up years. She was a large, black woman who loved us like her own children. We loved her and teased and always felt she was part of the family. She did laundry, cooked, cleaned, all the things my mother couldn't. I asked my mom about the coupon book.

"What are *you* doing with it?"

"She needed some help."

That's all she said. I looked through the payment book and discovered she had been paying on it the entire time. Six months later my mom and I visited Pauline in the hospital where she was dying, and she kept thanking my mom for all she had done for her. When you give, Jesus said, let your giving be in secret, and your Father who sees in secret will reward you (see Matthew 6:4). If his words were the caption, my mom was the picture that went with it.

SHE TAUGHT ME EVERYTHING . . .

Whatever I lost in a dad, I gained in a mom. She was the compensating grace in my life. She was like Job in a lot of ways. She hadn't deserved the disease or the divorce. Yet she refused to complain, much less to curse God. In spite of the pain, she carried on with love, with purpose, with dignity. She never gave up, never turned despondent.

Her hands couldn't iron my slacks or sew my shirts or tie my ties. She couldn't do much with them. Yet with them she taught me everything—a picture at a time, a blessing at a time.

"Hey . . . Dad . . . Wanna have a catch?"

Ray Kinsella

Field of Dreams

End of a Dream

It's my favorite scene from the movie *Field of Dreams*. The ending. Ray Kinsella's deceased father comes back as a young ballplayer to play on the field his son has built in that Iowa cornfield. Ray built the ballpark in response to that mysterious voice:

"If you build it, he will come."

Other messages come to Ray just as mysteriously as the first. "Ease his pain." "Go the distance." Ray becomes obsessed with trying to solve the meaning of these cryptic messages. Piece by piece the puzzle comes together. When the ballplayers from the 1919 White Sox team show up, Ray assumes the "he" the voice referred to is the star player, Shoeless Joe Jackson. What Ray discovers in the final scene is that the "he" is his father. And that the pain to be eased is Ray's. It is the pain of a washed-out bridge between a father and his son, the pain of words never spoken and words never heard.

When the father appears in that final scene, Ray receives a chance to start rebuilding that bridge.

"What do I say to him?" Ray asks his wife, Annie, as he sees his father on the field.

"Why don't you introduce him to his granddaughter?" she says.

Ray's father, John Kinsella, walks up to them. "Hi. Just wanted to thank you folks for putting up this field and letting us play here. I'm John," he says, extending his hand.

"I'm Ray," he says, shaking it. Ray turns to his daughter to introduce her to his father, but he stumbles over the words. "This is my . . . this is John."

"Hi, John," says his daughter, Karen.

"Very nice to meet you," says Annie.

"You catch a good game," says Ray.

"Thank you. It's so beautiful here. For me, for me it's like a dream come true. Can I ask you something? Is this heaven?"

"It's Iowa."

"Iowa? I could have sworn it was heaven," says John.

"Is there a heaven?"

"Oh, yeah," says John. "It's the place dreams come true."

Ray looks around and sees Annie and Karen on the porch. "Maybe this is heaven."

"Goodnight, Ray," his father says.

"Goodnight, John." The two shake hands, and the father walks off. But before he gets away, Ray calls to him, his voice cracking. "Hey . . . Dad . . . wanna have a catch?"

"I'd like that."

And the two toss the ball back and forth in casual arcs. As the sun goes down, Annie turns on the field lights. And as the camera lifts toward the horizon, we see a winding road of cars with their headlights on, all coming to see this field of dreams.

What a great scene. How I dreamed of such a scene with my own dad, a chance to speak those words, hear those words, a chance finally after all these years to ease my pain.

THE WORDS I LONGED TO HEAR

On a beautiful spring day in 1993, a secretary came running to my desk at work. "You need to get on the phone. It's the hospital!"

It turned out my father had just had a heart attack . . . *and had driven himself to the hospital.* The hospital staff had been trying to locate a next of kin and in his wallet found my card that I had given him several years before.

I called my older brother, Joe, and from different parts of the city we raced to St. Luke's Hospital. When we arrived, my father was strapped to a metal operating table. The IV drip had just been inserted, and he was prepped for surgery. Seeing us, the surgeon came over to talk.

"We're going to try to unclog the artery that collapsed during the angioplasty," he said. "There's a very good chance we'll lose him on the table." He paused. "I'll do all I can . . . but . . . if you've got something you want to say to your father, you'd better say it now."

We were given three minutes.

I patted Dad on the arm, telling him we loved him, that we were praying for him, that we'd be waiting when he got out of surgery. I read him a few verses I had scrawled on a small piece of paper in the lobby before coming up to his room. The verses were from Psalms. "I sought the LORD, and He answered me, and delivered me from all my fears. They looked to Him and were radiant, and their faces shall never be ashamed. This poor man cried and the LORD heard him, and saved him out of all his troubles. The angel of the LORD encamps around those who fear Him, and rescues them" (34:4-7).

I put the piece of paper into his hand. Then he looked up at Joe and me.

"Well, boys . . ."

There was a long pause.

"I guess I ought to say something."

Then an even longer pause.

We stood by his bedside, waiting. Not a word was spoken until a few minutes later when the nurses came and wheeled him away. As they did, he crumpled up the paper I had given him, letting it fall to the floor. Joe and I were left standing there, alone, as those cold, polished aluminum doors swung shut.

Ever since I first met my dad, I felt he had things he wanted to say but somehow couldn't. I kept waiting for those words to come. Hoping. Longing. Aching for those words. Maybe if he pulled through. Maybe then.

Dad had no money and no place to convalesce after his surgery, so we invited him to stay with us. I was almost forty, and it would be the first time we had spent the night under the same roof since I was two months old. I couldn't believe it. He was here, in my house, my very own dad. I was so excited, so hopeful.

For years I had tried to build a relationship with him. To bring out the warmth I knew had to be inside him somewhere. To learn what he'd been like as a child. To see if he was happy or if he was hurting over things in the past like I was. All of my attempts failed.

I had a thousand questions to ask him. As a counselor, I was good at asking questions. Even with the most resistant clients. Given enough time, I've always been able to get a person to open up. I was confident I could do the same with my dad.

During the six weeks he was at our house, I tried everything. Being direct. Being indirect. Giving him his space. Moving into his space. Trying to talk about what he felt comfortable talking about. But all he felt comfortable talking about was sports and the weather. Every time I tried to talk about family history, his life, spiritual things, he got angry. He'd shoot back a glare or a sharp remark or simply stiff-arm me with silence and retreat to his room.

Here we were under the same roof after all those years. Eating at the same table. Watching the same television. Sitting in the same living room. And yet we were so far apart, so many miles, so many years, so many experiences apart.

No matter what I tried or how hard I tried, he shut me out. I couldn't get to first base. Eventually he got worse. His heart and lungs were failing, and we finally had to put him in a hospice.

ONE FINAL CHANCE

On Sunday, August 9, my wife, Cindy, had just finished getting the girls dressed and fixing their hair. We started down the hall to get in the car for church when the phone rang. I picked it up.

"Dr. Trent, you'd better come to the hospice right away."

We all gathered in the hallway and prayed for "Grandpa." I sent them off to church, while I headed to the hospice . . . and one last chance to hear those words, to feel that embrace, to see something in his eyes, his smile, some hint that he cared, that I mattered, that he loved me, that he was sorry for all the missing years, sorry for all the pain, something.

For the next eight hours I sat holding my father's hand, listening to his desperate struggle for air, watching him slip away a breath at a time. I got him water, ice chips, another pillow, a blanket, whatever he needed or wanted. I spoke, but only when he wanted to talk. Except when the coughing spells got bad, and then I prayed for him, only to have him cuss me out for pushing Jesus on him. He never said a kind word to me the whole time. Never a word of thanks or love—nothing.

At 4:43 in the afternoon, he died.

So did something I had longed for all my life.

In the Old Testament, another twin named Esau suddenly realized he would never receive his father's blessing. We're told he "cried out with an exceedingly great and bitter cry, and said to his father, 'Bless me, even me also, O my father!'" (Genesis 27:34).

I knew how Esau felt. The very words he longed to hear from his father, I longed to hear from mine.

"Bless me, father. *Please.* Bless me."

I dreamed he would do that someday.

And that some day the two of us would have a catch.

"Nobody knows the trouble I've seen" goes the old spiritual, and of course nobody knows the trouble we have any of us seen—the hurt, the sadness, the bad mistakes, the crippling losses—but we know it. We are to remember it. And the happiness we have seen too—the precious times, the precious people.

Frederick Buechner

A Room Called Remember

Last Touch

Four years after my dad left the hospice, my mom entered it. Her room was just three doors down from his. There she spent the last four months of her life.

This day I was pacing the hall outside that room, a bright orange form in my hand, trying to put off the inevitable.

We had talked about it a dozen times over the years and especially in the months leading up to this day. Yesterday I had gone over the whole thing again with Mom's primary physician and the head nurse. And now *I* was the one who had to do it.

I was the one who had to walk into my mother's room, set that bright orange form in front of her, and have her sign it. It was the form reflecting her wish that there be no medical heroics in the last hours of her life.

It was the most difficult moment of my life.

Here sat my mother, my sweet, precious mother. Those bright, piercing eyes. Her thinning, snow-white hair. Her hands so warm and soft. We sat and held hands and talked. She was brave and courageous as ever.

I was a mess.

I cried at the thought of losing someone who had loved me and blessed me since the day I was born. A thousand memories washed over me. Of walks and hugs, of breakfasts at the old kitchen table, and of camping trips in our beat-up old trailer. The days watching the Dodgers in spring training. The midnight runs for my can collection. Late-night crackers. I couldn't keep the tears from my eyes as I thought of losing her listening ear, her gentle love, her precious life.

It was the worst day of my life. How many more days would we have her? Two, three, a week?

No Words Had Been Left Unspoken

Two weeks later, Joe and I were keeping vigil in her room. I was sitting in the chair, taking the first shift. He was sleeping in the bed next to her. At 2:20 in the morning her breathing grew shallow and irregular.

By now she had become so dehydrated she was unable to speak. But she didn't need to. She had said "I love you" hundreds of times with words and thousands of times with the pictures she left behind. No words needed to be spoken. No words needed to be heard.

As her breathing slowed, we moved our chairs next to her, one boy on each side, holding her hands. Hands that brushed away our tears and patted us gently when we had done well in sports or in school. Hands that put back so carefully the pieces of a broken heart. We nestled next to her just like when we were kids, when we got scared, or lonely, or just wanted to know that everything would be all right.

Only this time everything wouldn't be all right. This time she wouldn't be able to hug away the hurt.

Neither would we.

She breathed one last shallow breath. Neither Joe nor I moved. For several minutes we sat by her side, still and silent. Maybe if no one spoke, if no one stood up, if no one called the nurse, maybe somehow we could postpone the loss. Neither of us wanted to admit we had just lost our mother . . . and that we were now orphans.

I touched her hands for the last time. Those incredibly soft and tender hands.

I pray the first hands I see in heaven are the nail-scarred hands of my Savior.

And that the next ones I see are my mommy's.

Now straightened and strong.

But still soft and caring and lovely as I remembered them that day . . . and as I will remember them always.

The Pictures We Leave Behind

THE CANISTER AND RIFLE FIRE had ceased. The bombshells no longer flew. The Civil War had ended with the greatest loss of American lives in any war, even today. At Antietam, ten thousand were killed on both sides in a single *hour*. At Gettysburg, two thousand men charged across an open field and up a hill and less than three hundred struggled back alive.

Hundreds of thousands of brothers and cousins, fathers and sons lay in mass burial pits or individual graves.

Hundreds of thousands more had been terribly wounded.

The war was over. Now it was time for the nation to try to mend its wounds and recover from its incredible losses. But for all the talk about mending fences, it was also a time of great bitterness for many, from the men who woke up with nightmares of a best friend or brother killed right beside them to the overwhelming despair of a widow who had to raise a family alone to the mother and father who saw Johnny ride off in glory . . . and come home in pieces in a coffin.

There was just as much incentive to hate as to forgive.

Yet in the South, one man in particular took the lead in stressing reconciliation. Urging forgiveness. Personally working toward restoration. He was tireless in urging those who had fought for the Confederacy to pray daily for their former enemies, even as he did. He wrote literally hundreds of letters to his friends across the South, urging that there be no return to hostilities or unlawful rebellion under Reconstruction.

Who was this advocate of love, forgiveness, and responsibility? Probably a pastor. You'd expect that of course. Or a statesman seeking the "high road" that might lead his career upward as well. Some might have taken that political risk.

But this person wasn't a preacher or a politician.

The man urging forgiveness and reconciliation was . . . the Commanding General of the Confederacy.

You wouldn't expect that.

Yet Robert E. Lee took as active a role in reconciliation after defeat as he did in trying to lead his troops to victory. When asked to wear his military uniform for a parade, he refused, saying, "I am a soldier no longer." When a visiting clergyman began criticizing the North at a social gathering, Lee pulled the man aside, saying, "Doctor, there is a good old book which I read and you preach from which says, 'Love your enemies. Bless them that curse you, do good to them that hate you, pray for them which despitefully use you and persecute you.' Do you think your remarks this evening were quite in the spirit of that teaching? Since the War's end, I have never cherished towards them bitter or vindictive feelings, and have never seen the day when I did not pray for them."[1]

Bless . . . not curse. Do good . . . not carry hatred. Pray for them . . . even when they persecute you.

Incredible. Lee could have taken the lead in hating the North, yet he sought to bless. To heal. To mend. Until the day he died, he never stopped working for peace and restoration.

Wouldn't it be great to have the kind of faith where others marveled at our reactions and were moved by our choices to bless, not curse? Especially when it came to our choosing to count the positive pictures over the negative ones. Something General Lee did. Something I got to see my mother do, up close and personal.

I know many people who physically have suffered terribly, but I only lived with one. Someone who totaled many hours each day in discomfort, unmasked pain, and silent suffering. But she didn't curse, and rarely did she complain. She struggled with every step on two artificial ankles, two artificial knees, and one hip replacement (the same hip replaced two times). And that elbow replacement never quite worked.

That was just the physical pain. She could have been bitter enough about that. But there was also the pain that came in living in difficult times and circumstances. Losing two children to miscarriage before she had us boys. Being born on a dust bowl farm and living through the Great Depression. Having a husband who walked out on her and an alcoholic boss who taunted her. All those trials should have been more than enough to make her bitter. Toss in the physical suffering, and like the counsel of Job's wife, she should have cursed God and died. Yet she had Job's faith . . . not his wife's. On top of pictures of pain she was able, in spite of it all, to lay pictures of blessing.

I marveled at how focusing on the blessings in her life kept her spirit strong. How her love for the Lord kept growing and how her love for others was like sitting by the fire on a cold winter's night.

Robert E. Lee left pictures of reconciliation that the South did not forget. Closer to my home and history, my mom left pictures my brothers and I will never forget. And she left something else: a diary.

After her death I came across a priceless gift. Going through Mom's things, I found a small, handwritten diary. Not a day-by-day journal. In fact, in places a decade would go by before the next entry. But my eyes grabbed hold of the title she'd given it:

A Journal of Rededication to Jesus Christ

Here is her last journal entry. Spelling, capitals, and quotation marks are as she wrote them.

God is granting me yet another new beginning. There have been so many before. My hopes and dreams have been so high . . . but each time I fail. I call another driver STUPID. I make a cutting remark about another. I bring into a place of beauty discordant behavior, and thus foul up again.

But God has poured out blessings on me from the day of my birth. He has allowed me to live, "all the days of my life," at a time of great wonder, and in a State that dazzles the eyes and soul with beauty.

He has brought me a Teacher of His Word who is exceptional. He has provided me an annotated Bible, and so often restored my health.

All these plus the 3 miracles of creation who are my sons.

How blessed could one woman be?

Thank you, Lord. How inadequate is language to praise you.

You wouldn't expect a losing general to lead others in repentance and restoration. You wouldn't expect a crippled woman to overcome the pain and write words of praise.

But both did.

And both left lasting pictures on many people's lives as a result.

That's what this third section of the book is all about.

We've spoken of the pictures we've been left and the pictures we've been blessed with. Now it's time to get more personal. What about the pictures we'll leave behind? Will they be pictures of light or of darkness? Pictures of our praying for enemies or cursing them? Pictures that heal and leave hope or pictures that deepen and put salt in a wound?

What pictures will you leave behind that others will stumble across one day . . . and remember with fondness? What pictures will you leave that will touch lives and will inspire another to pray that he or she can do even half as well at loving God and choosing to live the blessing?

Magdalene College,
Cambridge
8/2/56

Dear Mary,
Thanks for your letter of the 2nd and for the Time cutting. My brother
says the photo of me is the best ever, but another friend says it is
unrecognisable. . . .

C. S. Lewis

Letters to an American Lady

NINETEEN

The Blessing Keeps On Blessing

In doing research for this book, I came across on the Internet a touching story that illustrates the importance of bringing light and life to the relationships around us. It's a true story, told by Sister Helen P. Mrosia, a nun who teaches in a Catholic school. It's about one of her students named Mark, and here is the story in her own words.

Mark talked incessantly. I had to remind him again and again that talking without permission wasn't acceptable. What impressed me so much, though, was his sincere response every time I corrected him. "Thank you for correcting me, Sister!" I didn't know what to make of it at first, but before long I grew accustomed to hearing it many times a day.

One morning when my patience was wearing thin, Mark talked once too often. I looked at him and said, "If you say one more word, I am going to tape your mouth shut!"

It wasn't ten seconds later when a student named Chuck blurted out, "Mark is talking again."

I hadn't asked any of the students to help me watch Mark, but since I had stated the punishment in front of the class, I felt I had to follow through. I walked to my desk, opened my drawer, and took out a roll of masking tape. Without saying a word, I walked to Mark's desk, tore off two pieces of tape, and made a big X with them over his mouth. When I returned to the front of the room, I glanced at Mark to see how he was doing, and he winked at me.

I started laughing. The class cheered as I walked back to Mark's desk, removed the tape, and shrugged my shoulders. His first words were, "Thank you for correcting me, Sister."

At the end of the year I was asked to teach junior high math. The years flew by, and before I knew it, Mark was in my classroom again. Since he had to listen carefully to my instructions in the "new math," he didn't talk as much in the ninth grade as he had in the third.

We had worked hard on a new concept all week, maybe a little too hard, and on Friday the students were frowning, frustrated with themselves and edgy with one another. I wanted to stop this crankiness before it got out of hand, so I gave the class a break from their math. Instead, I asked them to list the names of the other students in the room on two sheets of paper, leaving space between each name. Then I told them to think of the nicest thing they could say about each of their classmates and write it down.

It took the remainder of the class period to finish the assignment, and as the students left the room, each one handed me the papers. Charlie just smiled as he handed me his. And Mark said in his usual polite way, "Thank you for teaching me, Sister. Have a good weekend."

That Saturday I wrote down the name of each student on a separate sheet of paper, and I listed what everyone else had said about that individual. On Monday I gave each student his or her list. Before long, the entire class was smiling.

"Really?" I heard whispered.

"I never knew that meant anything to anyone!"

"I didn't know others liked me so much!"

No one ever mentioned those papers in class again. I never knew if they discussed them after class or with their parents, but it didn't matter. The exercise had accomplished its purpose. The students were happy with themselves and one another again.

That group of students moved on. Several years later, after I returned from vacation, my parents met me at the airport. As we were driving home, Mother asked me the usual questions about the trip—the weather, my experiences in general. Then there was a lull in the conversation. Mother gave Dad a sideways glance and said, "Dad?"

My father cleared his throat as he usually did before saying something important. "The Eklunds called last night," he began.

"Really?" I said. "I haven't heard from them in years. I wonder how Mark is."

Dad responded quietly. "Mark was killed in Vietnam," he said. "The funeral is tomorrow, and his parents would like it if you could attend."

I had never seen a serviceman in a military coffin before. Mark looked so handsome, so mature. All I could think at the moment was, *Mark, I would give all the masking tape in the world if only you would talk to me.*

The church was packed with Mark's friends. Chuck's sister sang "The Battle Hymn of the Republic." The pastor said the usual prayers, and the bugler played taps. One by one those who loved Mark took a last walk by the coffin and sprinkled it with holy water. I was the last one to bless it.

As I stood there, one of the soldiers who had served as pallbearer came up to me. "Were you Mark's math teacher?" he asked. I nodded as I continued to stare at the coffin. "Mark talked about you a lot," he said.

After the funeral, most of Mark's former classmates headed to Chuck's farmhouse for lunch. Mark's mother and father were there, waiting for me. "We want to show you something," his father said, taking a wallet out of his pocket. "They found this on Mark when he was killed. We thought you might recognize it."

Opening the billfold, he carefully removed two worn pieces of notebook paper that had obviously been taped, folded and refolded many times. I knew without looking that the papers were the ones on which I had listed all the good things each of Mark's classmates had said about him.

"Thank you so much for doing that," Mark's mother said. "As you can see, Mark treasured it."

Mark's classmates started to gather around us.

Charlie smiled sheepishly and said, "I still have my list. It's in the top drawer of my desk at home."

Chuck's wife said, "Chuck asked me to put his in our wedding album."

"I have mine, too," Marylin said. "It's in my diary."

Then Vicki, another classmate, reached into her pocketbook, took out her wallet, and showed her worn and frazzled list to the group. "I carry this with me at all times . . . I think we all saved our lists."

That's when I finally sat down and cried.

I cried for Mark.

And for all his friends who would never see him again.

THE BLESSING KEEPS ON LIVING

The pictures Sister Helen P. Mrosia left behind in the lives of her students brought light and life to those relationships. They never forgot her for it. Even while in Vietnam, Mark couldn't forget her. Couldn't forget the things she had taught him or the times she had corrected him. Couldn't forget the tape or how she laughed when he winked at her. And he couldn't forget the kindness of his classmates that shined through a Friday afternoon project she assigned.

"Mark talked about you a lot," the pallbearer said.

"They found this on Mark when he was killed," said Mark's father. "We thought you might recognize it."

"Thank you so much for doing that," Mark's mother said. "As you can see, Mark treasured it."

Can you see how the blessing keeps on blessing? A teacher who touched the life of a student touched the lives of the student's friends and the student's parents and who knows how many others. That is what's so wonderful about living the blessing. The blessing keeps living. Touching lives across the world, across the generations, and into eternity. Choosing to live the blessing is one of the most important decisions we can make with our lives. It begins with choosing Christ. And who knows where it will end . . . or what wonderful things will happen to you and through you along the way.

Along the way I've met a lot of people who have left behind blessings in my life. For them I am truly grateful. Along the way, too, some have left behind curses. For them I am sadly regretful. I forgive them, but I am sorry for them too. I'm sorry they've missed out on so much of what life has to offer. Sorry for whatever happened in their lives that brought death and darkness into them. Sorry that their deaths are mourned by so few.

My father's death was like that.

MOURNED BY FEW

His funeral was held in Phoenix at the National Veteran's Cemetery there. It was a desolate place, carved out of the desert. Outside of the immediate family, only one other couple came, and they came just to support the family. They had never met my dad.

Dad had told me he didn't want a funeral service, but when anyone is buried at the National Veteran's Cemetery, a chaplain and honor guard attend. When I told them Dad didn't want a service, they wanted to honor his wishes but still, it was military procedure, something they always did. So the chaplain spoke and three honor guards, men as old as my dad, fired twice into the desert sky. That was all. And we went home.

Six weeks after the funeral I had come in from jogging one morning and was walking down the hall when Kari came out of her room. This was unusual for two reasons. First, it was *really* early in the morning, and Kari is our "let's get up at the crack of noon" child. Second, instead of her usually cheery smile, she had huge tears rolling down her cheeks.

I fell to my knees and hugged her, and she fell into my arms, sobbing.

"Honey, what's wrong?"

"Oh, Daddy. I just realized that Grandpa's gone."

"I know it's hard," I said, trying to comfort her.

"But Daddy . . . *I never got to hug him.*"

When my father died, he hadn't even bothered to learn the name of our second daughter, Laura. He never picked up either of the girls. Never hugged them. Never held their hands. Nothing. And now the loss of all that is left behind in a little girl's heart.

I don't know why he never hugged us. Maybe his dad never hugged him. Maybe it went back for generations—silent, stoic men who never touched, never talked, never left pictures behind that blessed anybody. I didn't know how far back it went. But I knew this: It stopped here. I was going to make sure when I died there wouldn't be a grandchild left behind in a hallway, crying about the hugs that never happened.

Mourned by Many

My mom's funeral was different. She had picked her gravesite before she died, a place with a pond less than fifteen feet away. Five or six ducks landed on it during the service. Two swans swam with them. Such a contrast to my dad's gravesite. Hers had grass and trees and water. His was stark and treeless and dry. Two pictures that vividly captured the essence of their lives. The one, a blessing. The other, a curse.

When Mom died, we didn't have time to send her picture to the newspaper so only her name appeared in the obituaries. But that was enough. All sorts of people came. Three adopted sons came, people who had lived with us and whom my Mom had helped raise. People came from twenty-five years in her past, people she had encouraged in some way or befriended along the way. I don't have a large extended family, but every member was there. Her friends and coworkers were there. Her kids' friends. Grandkids. Over a hundred showed up that night for the memorial to pay their respects, including the football players from my high school.

After the funeral and the memorial, I was given the task of sorting through Mom's personal belongings. It was one of the hardest things I've ever done. The obvious things like her pictures and jewelry and computer had already been divided among us boys as she had wished, but there was still a small apartment full of things that had to go somewhere. I was supposed to decide what to keep, what to throw away, and what to put in a yard sale.

I wanted to keep it all. Her worn-out, blue sweater that had wrapped her little shoulders was worth a fortune to me. I had laid it across her dozens of times. The long, wooden dowel that she used to change channels on her television instead of the remote control. I picked it up, remembering it with a smile, remembering how she used to point at something on television, either in enthusiasm or disgust. How could I part with *that*? And that faded red footstool with its worn lettering, "A little help for little feet." We used it when we were kids to reach the sink so we could wash our faces. Since then she had kept it in her bathroom.

Everything she left behind was in some way a picture of blessing. And though she no longer lived, something of her lived in the sweater and the dowel and the faded red footstool . . . and in so many more pictures that lived on in me.

I love you, Mom.

Love your enemies, do good to those who hate you, bless those who curse you, pray for those who mistreat you.

Jesus

Luke 6:27-28

Even Our Enemies

O n March 4, 1861, with the nation on the brink of civil war, Abraham Lincoln was sworn into office as president of the United States. On a temporary platform at the east end of the Capitol, he stood to address a crowd of over twenty thousand people, all of them filled with apprehension about the prospects of war. Lincoln put on his steel-rimmed glasses and with his manuscript in hand read in a clear, distinct voice his inaugural address.

The president spoke passionately about preserving the Union. Representing both the northern and southern states at the time, he said: "We are not enemies, but friends. We must not be enemies. Though passion may have strained, it must not break, our bonds of affection."[1]

Powerful words. But the picture of the man who read them wasn't. He was a lean and somewhat unpresidential-looking lawyer from Illinois. A slender log of a man with rough-hewn features. Craggy nose. Gaunt cheeks. Not very impressive. Some, like Stanton, Lincoln's political opponent in the election, even made fun of his physical appearance. For a lot of people, the unimpressive picture didn't match the impressive words.

Until after the election.

One by one Lincoln filled his cabinet with men he trusted, men who not only understood his policies but who were eager to implement them. When the day finally came for him to choose that most critical post of secretary of war, the president chose Stanton. The uproar was immediate. His advisers tried to talk some sense into him. "Mr. President, you are making a mistake. Do you know this man Stanton? Are you familiar with all the ugly things he's said about you? He is your enemy. He will seek to sabotage your program. Have you thought this through, Mr. President?"

Lincoln's reply was brusque. "Yes, I know Mr. Stanton. I am aware of all the terrible things he has said about me. But after looking over the nation, I find he is the best man for the job."

Stanton, to his critics' surprise, was outstanding in the role, serving the president and the nation with distinction. Several years later, when the war was over and Lincoln was assassinated, powerful words in praise of the president were spoken in sermons, speeches, and eulogies. None of the words, however, were as powerful as those Stanton spoke as he stood near the dead body of the man he had once hated. He referred to Lincoln as one of the greatest men who ever lived and closed his remarks by saying, "He belongs to the ages now."

Lincoln lived his life trying to bring light and life to every relationship. Even his relationships with his enemies. He was often criticized for it. He spoke kindly not only *to* his enemies but *about* his enemies. Overhearing Lincoln say a kind word about the South, an infuriated bystander confronted him about it. "Madam," he answered, "do I not destroy my enemies when I make them my friends?"[2]

JESUS' PRINCIPLES FOR CHOOSING TO LIVE OUT THE BLESSING

"Love your enemies," Jesus said, "do good to those who hate you, bless those who curse you, pray for those who mistreat you."

Powerful words. But they were spoken, as Lincoln's were spoken, in the inaugural days, the early part of his ministry. Beautiful rhetoric. Lofty ideals. Impressive words. But spoken by an unimpressive man.

A man from Nazareth—and can any good thing come from there?

A man without formal education—and he's going to lecture *us*?

A man of questionable parentage—have you heard the rumors?

A man with a questionable peer group—have you seen the parties he goes to?

No. The picture doesn't really fit the words. Yet the words are so powerful. Luke 6 records the entire address. In it are the choices we need to make if we are to bring light and life to our relationships, especially the most difficult ones.

The Principle of Blessing Difficult Relationships

Love your enemies, do good to those who hate you, bless those who curse you, pray for those who mistreat you. (vv. 27-28)

The Specifics of Blessing Difficult Relationships

Whoever hits you on the cheek, offer him the other also; and whoever takes away your coat, do not withhold your shirt from him either. Give to everyone who asks of you, and whoever takes away what is yours, do not demand it back. And just as you want people to treat you, treat them in the same way. (vv. 29-31)

The Reason for Blessing Difficult Relationships

And if you love those who love you, what credit is that to you? For even sinners love those who love them. And if you do good to those who do good to you, what credit is that to you? For even sinners do the same. And if you lend to those from whom you expect to receive, what credit is that to you? Even sinners lend to sinners, in order to receive back the same amount. But love your enemies, and do good, and lend, expecting nothing in return; and your reward will be great, and you will be sons of the Most High; for He Himself is kind to ungrateful and evil men. (vv. 32-35)

The Principle of Blessing Difficult Relationships Summarized

Be merciful, just as your Father is merciful. (v. 36)

The Benefits of Blessing Difficult Relationships

And do not judge and you will not be judged; and do not
condemn, and you will not be condemned; pardon, and you will
be pardoned. Give, and it will be given to you; good measure,
pressed down, shaken together, running over, they will pour into
your lap. For by your standard of measure it will be measured to
you in return. (vv. 37-38)

They are some of the most powerful words in all the Bible. And if we apply them, they will give light to the relationships that have been lost to the
darkness . . . and life to those we have given up all hope of ever resurrecting.

The words Jesus first spoke in his inaugural sermon were powerful words.

They are the words of a caption in search of pictures—pictures lived out
in your life and mine.

WASHINGTON—Hundreds of thousands of praying, singing and somewhat tearful men blanketed the National Mall on Saturday for a giant service of prayer and atonement organized by the Denver-based evangelical group Promise Keepers.

Although there was no official crowd estimate, the six-hour gathering appeared to be one of the largest religious events ever recorded in the United States.

Adriel Bettelheim

The Denver Post, Sunday, October 5, 1997

Twenty-One

It Starts on Our Knees

I t was a picture-perfect day, sunny and warm, with fall colors tinting the foliage. I'll never forget it. It was a Saturday. October 4, 1997. It was the day over a million men converged on the nation's capital.

I stood on a scaffold twenty feet above the ground observing the event. From there I could see that the crowd stretched from a stage across from the Capitol to the Lincoln Memorial nearly three miles away. They stood there for six hours. It was an awesome sight. The men came from every state, every denomination, every race. They came not to picket or protest. They came to pray, to ask forgiveness for the past, and to make a commitment for the future.

They call themselves "Promise Keepers." They are men who want to be good husbands, good fathers, good men. Men who keep their promises.

They realize, like the alcoholic in recovery, that they can't do it on their own. That's why they knelt on the grassy Washington Mall. A million men kneeling together to pray.

The picture brought tears to my eyes. And a reminder. *This is where it starts: on our knees.* This is where we must go, day in, day out, if we are to be people of blessing. We can't do it on our own. We need grace to look at the pictures from our past. We need grace to understand them. Grace to feel compassion for them. And if needed, grace upon grace to forgive them.

God gives grace to the humble, the Scriptures tell us. The place the humble go to receive that grace is on their knees. That is where we need to go not only to process the pictures we're left with but to produce the pictures we're wanting to leave behind.

31 Days to Living the Blessing

HAVE YOU EVER dressed up the kids, driven to a studio, and taken a family portrait? It can be a traumatic experience to get everyone stuffed into those uncomfortable dress clothes, much less have them sit still and smile at the same time.

But just as difficult can be going back to look at the proofs.

You wait several weeks.

Come back to the studio.

Then they open up the folder and lay out what you *really* looked like that day. And it's not always the picture you want.

But it's also not the picture you *have* to hang on the wall. That's why it's called a proof. In fact, our family has been known to fail to have a single proof with everyone's eyes open and heads turned the same way. We've even had to retake a portrait to get it right. But we've gone through all that trouble because we know the final version is so *permanent.*

That's what I want to encourage you to do in this section.

Choosing to live out the blessing creates pictures; you've clearly seen that. But unless this is your last day on earth, those pictures can be proofs.

Perhaps we've failed in the past to bless and affirm. *We can change that picture.*

Perhaps we've been missing from the family photo album or seen anger or bitterness eat away at the edges. *We can change the picture.*

For many of us, all it will take is a touch-up. For others it may take more, perhaps even an appointment with a pastor or Christian professional to help us sort through the hurt and talk through the pain.

But for each of us, we can choose to live out the blessing. Even if we're in process. Even if the pictures we've left behind haven't been the best.

And the best way I could think of to help you do this was to provide a way to make the blessing a conscious, daily habit.

In the pages that follow, you'll find thirty-one days of devotionals, along with questions for discussion and daily thought and application. It's been said that it takes at least twenty-one days for something to become a habit. I think for most of us, a few more days (or even a lifetime) would help to ingrain the choice to bless others in our minds and hearts.

These devotionals can help you think through, pray through, and apply what you've learned. They're broken into four sections, each with daily readings—four sections to walk you back through the high points of what you've read in this book and to encourage you to make the blessing a daily, purposeful practice:

First Steps to Blessing Others (Days 1 through 7)

Bless, Rather Than Curse (Days 8 through 14)

Bless, O Lord, My Family (Days 15 through 25)

Bless, O Lord, the Way I Live My Life (Days 26 through 31)

So prayerfully consider taking this book with you to work or on that trip or placing it on your pillow in the morning so at night you have to pick it up. It would be wonderful to involve your family and use these 31 Days of Blessing as a daily family devotional at the dinner table or at breakfast. Or make a commitment with your spouse to read through one short session each night, discussing the questions that follow each day's comments.

Think what could happen in your home if for the next thirty-one days you make blessing others a main focus? A purposeful choice. A matter of prayer and commitment.

In fact, I'd love to hear from you about your experiences after you've chosen to live out the blessing for thirty-one days. It can be a short note that's a prayer request or a lengthy praise report I could share with others. It could recount your personal journey or what you've learned as a couple or family or even as a Sunday school or Bible study class.

Most of all, I pray that as this wonderful concept of the blessing becomes more a part of your life you'll see your relationships more filled with light and love than ever before. So bright, in fact, that your friends, neighbors, and coworkers will be drawn themselves to the Source of your warmth and love.

May the Lord bless, keep, and guide you and yours each day of your life.

John Trent, Ph.D.
Encouraging Words
12629 North Tatum Boulevard, Suite 208
Phoenix, Arizona 85032

First Steps to Blessing Others

Memory! What a gift of God. And what a tragedy at times. Memory can be of horrible things one wants to forget, coming at times like a nightmare bringing trembling and horror, or memory can be of wonderful things one enjoys living and reliving. Memory can bring sudden understanding later in life when things suddenly fall into place and you realize what was happening, and memory can give you courage to go on—just when it is needed. Memory can quiet in time of turmoil or can transport one out of the danger of being plunged into something false. Memory can suddenly become so vivid as to stop a person from doing something wrong—because of the unmistakable contrast being flashed on the screen of the mind—and memory can cause someone to be compassionate to another in need, whose need would not have been noticed had it not been linked in the mind's picture with a deep experience in the past which prepared an understanding.

Edith Schaeffer, *What Is a Family?*

The power of memory is that it lives. It lives to give light or to take it away, to enhance our lives or diminish them, to bless us or to curse us.

Think back to a picture in your past that blessed you. Maybe it was the picture of a teacher who encouraged you or a parent who trusted you or a friend who helped you. What was it about the picture that blessed you? What did the picture say to you? How did it make you feel?

Now think about the people in your life today—a parent, child, friend, mate, teacher, coworker. How can you pass to them the picture of blessing that was passed to you?

Think visually. Think specifically. And think today.

What can you do *today* to bring a blessing to someone's life?

You can smile a little more. That's a good place to start. You can make a phone call to someone who's been on your mind lately. Or write a thank-you note to someone whose life has meant a lot to you but you've never taken the time to say it. You can take a walk with someone during your lunch break, using the time to share something of your life or to ask that your companion share from his or her life. You can fix a snack to share and while eating it express appreciation for something about that person. Call a friend and ask if there's anything you can be praying for. Or share your own concerns and ask the friend to pray for you.

There are lots of ways to get started. The place you start is not nearly as important as the time.

Don't let another page get turned on the calendar without leaving a picture of blessing in the life of someone you love.

Start today.

Lord, there have been so many "I'll start tomorrow's" in my life. Starting TODAY, let me each day for the next thirty-one days live out your blessing in a world full of darkness.

(Thoughts and questions for reflection and discussion:)

A picture in the past that has blessed me is a picture of . . .

One thing I could do today to bless and encourage just one other person would be to . . .

Day 2

There is a delightful little children's book that expresses some tender and poignant thoughts about what we've been discussing in this book. It's titled *The Memory Box*, written by Mary Bahr and illustrated by David

Cunningham. It's the story of a boy's relationship with his grandfather. When the grandfather learned he had Alzheimer's disease, he wanted to make sure the important memories wouldn't be forgotten, which was the catalyst for the idea of the Memory Box.

"It was your Great-Gram who told me about the Memory Box," Gramps said, staring at the sunset sky. "It's a special box that stores family tales and traditions. An old person and a young person fill the box together. Then they store it in a place of honor. No matter what happens to the old person, the memories are saved forever."

During the grandson's vacation, the two of them remembered everything they could. The times they fished together and picked blueberries together. The time they watched as a raccoon ate a tray full of cookies Gram had set on the picnic table to cool.

It was Grampa's job to add photos and souvenirs to the Memory Box. He found a picture of my second birthday party when I had taken a bite off the top of the cake. There was a shot of Gram in her wedding dress with flowers in her hair and one of Dad in his football uniform when he still had hair. Another was of Gramps and Mom the day he had taught her to ride a bike. She had ridden it too. Right over his foot!

As the summer progressed, so did the Alzheimer's. The grandfather began to forget things, get lost in the woods, talk to people who weren't there. One minute he seemed fine; another minute he might be reliving a day of his childhood. As he deteriorated, the Memory Box became more important to both of them.

When Gramps woke up, he called me. I stood at his bedroom door. He sat on the bed.
  "Did Gram tell you about this useless old man? And how he

needs to find a home for special things like this?" He handed me the old fishing knife from the shed. "I forgot the sheath, so I went back . . . and got lost."

"Thanks," I whispered, holding the knife the way Gramps had taught me. My own, very first knife. I'd always wanted one. This one.

But now it didn't seem so important.

"Your Mom's going to hurt," Gramps said. "When it gets bad, bring out the Memory Box. Show her what I remember."

Summer vacation ended, and it was time for the boy to return home. He hugged his grandparents good-bye. He hugged his grandpa especially hard. And when his grandma hugged him, she turned her head to his ear.

"Add things to the Memory Box you want Gramps to remember," she whispered as she handed it to me. "And bring it with you next summer. We'll need it, you and I."

The boy's parents came to take him home. When they drove off, the boy waved to his grandparents, thinking about his summer there and already looking forward to the next. The book ends with a final thought from the boy.

As the car hit the top of the hill, I watched Gramps slowly disappear into the horizon. And I hugged my Memory Box.

Precious Savior, thank you that when our eyes grow dim and memories fade, you don't forget. You remember our smiles, the ragged steps we took in trying to follow you. Most of all you'll always remember our names. Because of Jesus, it's written in your most precious "memory box"—the Lamb's Book of Life.

Yesterday you were asked to recall a positive picture from your own "memory box." Today, ask your spouse or a close friend or your children to open their box of pictures of you.

Ask them, "What's one memory the two of us share that you'll always keep in your memory box?"

As you recall this moment with them—and don't be surprised if it's one you never would have picked or perhaps even remembered—give God thanks for that positive picture.

May the Lord grant you many, many more.

Day 3

How you photograph your loved ones, friends, and strangers can also reveal something about you.

Do you find that your favorite pictures of people show them in a vast landscape that causes your subjects to appear small and diminished? Perhaps compositions of this type reflect your own inner struggle with feeling overwhelmed by life or just how lonely life can be. Alternatively, these images might strike a positive note because they reflect your love of solitude. Do you find yourself shooting mostly faces? Such compositions might reflect the great compassion you're blessed with as well as your ability to freely interact with people. The reasons why you do what you do are numerous and in part define who you are, but photographs—unlike any other medium—can say volumes about you and the subjects you shoot in a single stroke.

Bryan Peterson, *People in Focus: How to Photograph Anyone, Anywhere*

In the same way that you are leaving pictures, you are also taking pictures. Those pictures form an album of what you view as important.

How much of that album contains pictures of people?

How would the people in your life feel if they looked through your album and saw it was mostly pictures of Monday Night football or Saturday golf, pictures of the fish you caught or your flower garden, or pictures of your furniture or jewelry?

When you *have* taken pictures of the people in your life, what do they reveal about how you view them?

Look at the pictures you have collected over the years. Are the subjects distant? Are the poses stiff?

And where is the focus? Is it on the surroundings? Is it on the lighting you're trying to capture or the mood you're trying to create?

Or is the focus on the people? On the faces of those you love. On their eyes. Their smiles. Their hearts.

Are you close enough to them even to see those things? To *really* see them?

If not, try moving in a little closer.

And do whatever you can to make them smile.

Lord, how easy it is to put people—even my precious family—
into the background. To put a television set, or a spy or
romance novel, or the quest for a promotion, or even a golf
club or computer game in the foreground instead of having my
friends and family there—or YOU there.

Lord, I love the people in my life. I love You. But I've
taken so many pictures where the most important things were
standing in the background, like so much rented scenery. That's
not the blessing. Lord Jesus, forgive me. And teach me to be
there, each day, to put first things front and center.

Ask yourself the following questions—honestly:

If a film crew had followed me around the past twenty-four hours, what would they have seen—really?

Were people and the Lord front and center? Or were they pushed into the background?

Day 4

According to a story recently making the Internet rounds, a New York teacher wanted to honor her senior high students, and she did so by telling each of them the difference their lives had made. Using a process developed by a California woman named Helice Bridges, she called the students one at a time to the front of the class. She told them specifically how they had made a difference in her life and in the lives of the other students. Then she gave each of them a blue ribbon with gold letters that read "Who I Am Makes a Difference."

Afterward, as a class project she decided to see what kind of impact this recognition might have on a community. She gave the students three ribbons each and told them to honor others in the same way they had been honored. In a week they were to report on the results.

One of the students went to a junior executive in a company, pinned the ribbon on his shirt, and told him how much he appreciated the man taking the time to help him plan his career. He gave the man the remaining two ribbons and explained, "We're doing a class project on recognition, and we'd like you to find someone to honor, give him or her one of the ribbons and have that person give away the other ribbon to someone he or she would like to honor. When you're finished, let me know what happened so I can report back to the class."

Later that day the junior executive stepped into the office of his boss, a man known for his gruffness. He told his boss how much he admired him for being a creative genius. The boss was surprised. Then the junior executive asked if he would accept the blue ribbon and let him pin it to the boss's coat, right above the heart. The boss was even more surprised, but he agreed. Then the junior executive asked, "Would you do me a favor? Would you take this extra ribbon and pass it on to someone else that you would like to honor? The young boy who first gave me the ribbons is doing a school project and wanted to keep this recognition ceremony going to find out what effect it has on the people who receive it."

That night the boss came home and sat down with his fourteen-year-old son. He said, "The most incredible thing happened to me today. I was in my office, and one of the junior executives came in and told me he admired me and gave me a blue ribbon for being a creative genius. Imagine. He thinks I'm a creative genius. Then he pinned the ribbon on my jacket, above my heart. It says, 'Who I Am Makes a Difference.' He gave me an extra ribbon and asked me to find somebody else to honor. As I was driving home, I was thinking about who I would give it to, and I thought about you. I want to honor you, Son. My days are really hectic, and when I come home, I don't pay a lot of attention to you. Sometimes I scream at you for not getting good enough grades or for leaving your room in a mess. But tonight I just want to sit here and, well, let you know that you do make a difference. Besides your mother, you are the most important person in my life. You're a great kid, and I love you!"

The boy started crying; his body started shaking. He wept uncontrollably. Finally through his tears, he looked up and said, "I was planning to commit suicide tomorrow, Dad, because I didn't think you loved me. Now I don't need to."

Dear Lord, there is so much darkness. And when the soul feels empty and rejected, sometimes even good people can contemplate death. Like Elijah. Like Moses.

If the truth be known, maybe someone close to me . . . even me.

But you know that, Lord. How desperate we can get. How hopeless the world can look. And yet you also know how words of blessing can provide a ray of hope and a lifeline out of that despair.

Help me realize this, Lord, and to speak those words.

I know I can't chase away all the darkness in the world, but today I'm committed to bless _____ with spoken words to help light his or her way.

Day 5

My wife and I once asked a group of older people to think of one autobiographical object from their past. They were to write it down in big letters on a sheet of paper, pin the paper on their chest, and walk around the room. Pretty soon they were sporting signs, saying "buttonhook," "old-fashioned pen," "match," "fishing pole," "Hershey Bar," "tricycle," and much more. . . .

One of the women had written "coral elephant" on her piece of paper. She had come from a poor family that couldn't afford new clothes or jewelry for its children. Around the sixth grade, the girl became fascinated with a teacher, a young, attractive woman who always wore beautiful things. One day it was a piece of jewelry, a coral elephant pin, and throughout the day the girl couldn't take her eyes off it. After school she lingered to get a better look and tell the teacher how pretty it was. At the end of the school year, the teacher gave the girl that pin. "It was my most prized possession," the woman said with tears in her eyes. And yet, several years ago, she lost it in a move. All she has left is its memory, and a story that could symbolize her life.

John Kotre, *White Gloves: How We Create Ourselves Through Memory*

One of the most powerful things about a picture is that it symbolizes something. Here, a pin symbolizes a teacher's fondness for her student and her student's for her. It was prized when the girl first received it. As she grew older, it was prized even more. So much so, that years later the mere memory of it brought tears.

When the person that the object symbolizes is gone, the symbol keeps talking, keeps reminding us of the relationship and how it has shaped us and is shaping us still.

How is the language of your heart being translated? What objects in your relationship with others symbolize what the relationship means to you?

A bowl of ice cream? A box of chocolates?

A game of racquetball? A Saturday of garage sales?

A board game? A music box?

When you're gone, what symbols will be left behind to carry on the conversation?

Dear Heavenly Father, it's amazing how we who have so much still want more and more. And yet how little it really takes for someone to feel loved, blessed, honored. Thank you for that picture of a tiny elephant which left such a big impression on a little life. Remind me, Lord, that the smallest act of kindness I do today can carve out a lasting memory for someone tomorrow.

Look around your home. Pick out one thing that truly *means* something to you. Don't pick something because of its price or size but because it's a symbol of someone who blessed you at some time in your life. Share the importance of that object with a loved one or close friend.

Day 6

This week you've read about leaving positive memories, about being people-focused instead of thing-focused, and about how the smallest act of kindness can leave an unforgettable blessing. Today we'll look at yet another foundational aspect of the blessing.

Certainly we bless people by loving them as our Lord loves. Yet we need to *know* someone in order to bless that person. Think of how Jesus selected his disciples and spent time with them and *knew* them. He knew their smiles as well as their struggles, what made them happy as well as their hurts. And so should we, as people of blessing.

The story is told of a Hassidic rabbi who was poring over a book when one of his students approached him and in a burst of emotion proclaimed, "Master, I love you!"

The old rabbi looked up and asked, "Do you know what hurts me, my son?"

The young man looked puzzled. "I don't understand the question, Rabbi. I am trying to tell you how much you mean to me, and you confuse me with irrelevant questions."

"My question is neither confusing nor irrelevant," replied the rabbi. "For if you don't know what hurts me, how can you truly love me?"

It's a good question. A profound question actually. And maybe a question we should live with for a while.

Make a mental list of the people you love.

Now list their hurts.

Did you come up short on the hurt list?

If you don't know what hurts them, how can you truly love them?

Think again, this time praying with a specific person in mind, asking the Holy Spirit to reveal some of the hurts that are hidden to your eye. Start with the prayer below, adding to it words of your own. Then wait. Silently. Humbly. Expectantly. And maybe God will reveal something that will help you love that person more truly.

Help me to love _____, Lord. To do that, to
truly do that, I have to know what hurts _____. But
perhaps because of my own insensitivity or because we're all so
good at hiding our hurts, I don't know what hurts _____.
Help me to see, ask, and understand what does. How have

his/her hurts shaped _____? Or misshaped _____? And
what can I do about it? How can I pray, how can I bring
healing, how can I truly love this person? Show me, Lord.

Day 7

In her book *What Is a Family?* Edith Schaeffer says a family should be a museum of memories. "Memories ought to be planned, memories ought to be chosen, memories ought to be put into the budget, memories ought to be recognized and given the proper amount of time, memories ought to be protected, memories ought not to be wasted, and memories ought to be passed down to the next generation."

Here is a story illustrating how that is done. The story is told by Gladys Hunt. I hope it will stimulate your thoughts about the memories you're passing down to the next generation.

My grandfather was a Dutch immigrant with ten children. He and
my grandmother took seriously the instructions given by God in
Deuteronomy 6, believing this to be a Christian parent's
responsibility:

"These words which I command you this day shall be upon your
heart; and you shall teach them diligently to your children, and
shall talk of them when you sit in your house, and when you lie
down, and when you rise."

As the family gathered around the table for meals, one of my
grandparents read from the Bible, usually three times a day. It was a
kind of spiritual dessert. They had enjoyed physical food from the
hand of God; now they would enjoy spiritual food.

My father was one of these children. Later, when four small offspring sat around his table, he initiated the same practice. (As far as I know, his brothers and sisters have done similarly in their homes.) We never discussed whether or not we wanted to do this; it was just always done and never, to my knowledge, questioned. Reading material was chosen according to our ages. Often at this evening meal we read from a Bible storybook, but at least once a day we read short selections from the Bible. For some reason we read Proverbs more than any other single book; my parents must have believed that book contained an extraordinary amount of wisdom for everyday living.

To the children in our family this was a logical thing for a Christian family to do. No one left the table, unless for special reasons, until we read the Scriptures together. This was no legalistic ritual; it was family habit. Thinking back, I remember numerous instances when our friends called for us and we asked them to wait until we had finished dinner. Dessert may have been served, but none of us ever considered the meal finished until we had read together.

As I recounted this to a group of young couples recently, one father asked me, "Didn't you all grow up resenting your father and Christianity?" I felt an aching kind of amusement at his question.

"Quite the other way around," I answered. In all honesty, our parents and memories of family life are extra dear because of this.

Dear Lord, wouldn't it be great if every child in every home heard your Word at every meal? Before devouring the mashed potatoes or spilling their milk, they received a picture of what nourishes their soul? They heard of a heavenly meal, which after partaking of we never hunger nor thirst? A picture of you,

Lord Jesus. Our Savior. Our Redeemer. The blessing, in human form.

You've spent a full week seeking to live out the blessing. Perhaps you've chosen to use spoken words or hugs or letters or a priceless verse to communicate God's good gift.

Take a moment to ask yourself, "What has this week taught me about blessing others?" Jot down these thoughts, or share them with someone close to you.

What has been hard as you seek to live out the blessing?

What has been helpful to you or to others?

What can you thank the Lord for?

Bless, Rather Than Curse

Day 8

If you spent last week trying to live out the blessing, then I'm almost certain you've already faced this week's focus—barriers to blessing others. Like Peter, our desire may be strong, but our flesh is weak. Far too weak to try to live out the blessing in our own strength, apart from his Spirit. This is particularly true when we carry around hurts that can cause us to lash out at others, even those we love.

> *A thirteen-year-old boy and his younger sister had had a disagreement over who got to use the home computer one evening and the boy slapped her. The father grabbed him by the shoulders and demanded, "Why did you do that, son?"*
>
> *Now, that's usually not a very good question to ask children, particularly younger ones. We will ask something like, "Why did you pour out that cereal?" and of course the kid doesn't know why he did it.*
>
> *But with this boy the question was more meaningful. The father really did wonder why he had done it, and so did the boy. He was not usually physical, especially with his sister. No answer came to him, though, and he only said, "I'm sorry."*
>
> *About an hour later the boy came to his dad and said, "I've been thinking about your question and I think I know the answer."*
>
> *The father looked at his son, obviously proud of him, and asked him to go on.*
>
> *"Well," said the boy, "I went to my room to think about it, and*

I remembered that my math teacher embarrassed me in front of the whole class today. I was so mad at her, but I couldn't do anything about it, so I just kept all those bad feelings inside of me all day. I think I just let them out at Sis."

Linda and Richard Eyre, *Teaching Your Children Sensitivity*

When we are left with a picture like the one the math teacher left, it affects the pictures *we* leave behind. When we are hurt, we get angry. And even though we try our best to keep the anger in, we can't. Not for long, anyway. It's like trying to keep a beachball underwater. The more determined we are to push it down, the more forceful it is in pushing its way up.

Take a few minutes to think about the pictures you've left behind. Did any of those pictures embarrass anyone, humiliate anyone, demean anyone? It doesn't take much. A defiant gesture. A disgusted look. A sarcastic word.

If you've left a picture like that in someone's life, go to that person and talk about it. Ask her what she saw, what she heard, how she felt. Tell her—or him—how sorry you are for what you said, for what you did, for how you reacted.

Look at it as a chance to touch up a really tacky photograph and turn a blemish into a blessing.

Oh, Jesus. How patient you are with my desire to retaliate and hold on to those terrible pictures from the past. Not to keep me humble or make me more dependent on you but to exact revenge or as an incentive to work harder to "show them" they were wrong. That's not right, Lord. I know it. I know I'll never truly be a person of blessing if I don't lay the bad pictures at your cross.

What is a negative picture from *the last six months* that you've had a hard time letting go of? Write it down. Ponder it. Pray over it. Lay it down at his cross so you're ready to pick up his love to bless others.

Day 9

The Kilns
6 July 63

Dear Mary,

. . . *Do you know, only a few weeks ago I realised suddenly that I at last had forgiven the cruel schoolmaster who so darkened my childhood. I'd been trying to do it for years; and like you, each time I thought I'd done it, I found, after a week or so it all had to be attempted over again. But this time I feel sure it is the real thing. And (like learning to swim or to ride a bicycle) the moment it does happen it seems so easy and you wonder why on earth you didn't do it earlier . . . .*

Yours,
Jack

The letter was written by C. S. Lewis, noted Christian author and apologist, to an American woman he had met through a letter. During the course of more than a hundred subsequent letters, they carried on a friendship. The friendship continued for thirteen years; this letter was written just a few months before he died. In it he recounts the painful childhood memory of a teacher in an English public school who bullied him and all the other boys in his class.

The hurt little boy grew up to be a teacher himself, a well-respected scholar at a well-respected university. He was a famous author, writing letters to people across continents to help them as they struggled with their faith. And he was a strong Christian. Yet it took him all his life to come to terms with that picture.

The pictures teachers leave behind are some of the most powerful in our lives.

Each of us is a teacher in somebody's life. Whether we're parents helping children with their homework. Whether we're coaches teaching athletes teamwork. Whether we give piano lessons or volunteer for vacation Bible school. Whether den mothers or scoutmasters, we are all teachers.

The pictures we leave have the power to enlighten others or, as in Lewis's case, to bring darkness. And the darkness may follow them, as it did him, all of their lives.

Take a minute to thumb through the pictures of your past. Do you have a picture like the one Lewis had? If so, ask God to shed light on the picture, enabling you to see it through more compassionate eyes. Then take the picture to the cross, forgiving as Jesus forgave, entrusting the injustice, as he did, to him who judges righteously.

Lord, I'm back again. I know that just yesterday I was praying over a picture that hurt me. That one was of recent origin. But, Lord, you know I've got others. Some that go all the way back to my grade school days or growing up at home. Those pictures still hurt and often hold me back from blessing others. I bring them before you as well. Thank you, Lord, for cleansing me from the inside out that I might love you and others more.

Yesterday's picture of hurt or pain was in the recent past. What picture have you hung on to for years? What other picture needs to be laid at the cross as well?

Day 10

There is a popular black-and-white photograph that shows a little boy and girl from the back, holding hands as they are walking out of a dark leafy tunnel and into the shimmering light. If you think a minute, I'm sure you'll remember seeing it somewhere.

The father of the children, W. Eugene Smith, took the picture.
For police officer Lucille Burrascano, it's her favorite. Here's why.

"He took these children out of a tunnel-effect into the light, two
children walking together down the road of life. This is his beautiful
wish for joy and lightness and happiness.

"It's about the future. They're in motion, and they're hand in
hand. When I was working with abused children, this image
became even more profound to me, because abused children aren't
allowed to be like this. This picture became my goal. . . .

"For abused children, life is always a tunnel. There's never any
light. . . . They are locked into anger and bitterness and fear, and
can't go forward. What I love about this picture is that these two
children, the two inarticulate adults, these midgets, have taken that
step and come out of the darkness. . . .

"Make this picture a goal, I say. Let your child go forward
unscattered, unfettered, unscathed. There's going to be enough chaos
in their lives. There's going to be enough tragedy, God knows, it's out
there. I tell the mothers, 'Now go home and kiss your babies good
night. Go out and save some children. They're not going to be babies
forever.'"

Lucille Burrascano, quoted in *Talking Pictures: People Speak About the Photographs*
That Speak to Them by Marvin Heiferman and Carole Kismaric

It's easy to look at the photograph of the boy and girl holding hands as
they emerge from the tunnel of leaves and see how it relates to children. But
there are tunnels in life through which each of us may someday have to pass.
A long tunnel of addiction. A leafy tunnel of changing jobs, changing neighborhoods, changing friends. A dark tunnel of disease, divorce, death.

How do we get through them?

No matter how long or how dark the tunnel or how confusing the turns
along the way, the surest way to get through is to follow the light. The safest
way is to take each other's hand.

Do you have a picture in your mind of somebody who is trapped in a tunnel, somebody who's a little lonely, a little lost, a little scared? Step into the photo, won't you? Take his hand. Walk through it with her. Your companionship through this difficult passage in life will be a picture he or she will never forget.

Lord, I've been in those tunnels. A period of time and trial that seemed to stretch out forever. Where the pain seemed all around me and the light so far away. Father, even if I'm there now, let me remember someone today who's in the midst of his or her own tunnel . . . and seek to light the way.

The person the Lord brings to mind today who could use my blessing is . . .

What could I do today to step into this person's tunnel and give him or her a picture of hope?

Day 11

Pictures our children see make an impact on them. So do the ones they don't see. Like the one in the following poem. When you've finished reading it, pause to reflect on the pictures you're *not* leaving in the lives of those who are watching. Like the people who work at one of your favorite restaurants, where you leave a gratuity behind but no gratitude. No 10 percent in your words. No 15 percent on your face. No 20 percent in your eyes. When you finish the poem, think of them. And think of all they're not getting . . . because you haven't left it.

"mommie," she says, "i've never seen you and daddy kiss."
"of course you have," the mother says,
"you've just forgotten."

"i wouldn't have forgotten that," she says,
"because I always wish you would."

"it doesn't matter," her father says. "we
both love you and we love each other in our
own way."

"you've seen us kiss," the mother says.

"not on the mouth, not the way people
kiss on your soap operas."

"your mother and i have been together
nearly twenty years," her father says.
"we did a lot of kissing in our time.
that's why we have you and your brother,
thank god."

"maybe you did, but you don't now,"
their daughter says.

the father says, "your mother and i sleep
in the same bed. we do our best to get along
and we have our love for you and your brother
in common. there are things we have come to
understand that you will someday understand."

this almost satisfies her, but she adds,
"i think you wish that mommie still kissed you."

the mother says, "if you're finished eating,
you may leave the table."

Gerald Locklin, "Learning to See Crooked"

Lord, what are the little ones (or the grown-up ones) seeing
when they look at me? At us? Love? Blessing? Affection?
Caring? Or do they see anger? Alienation? Indifference?

> *Disrespect? I know blessing others starts at home, Lord. I know.*
> *But it's not enough just to know. Help me do the things I know*
> *bring light to my home.*

Anger, difficulty in forgiving, tunnels of despair, and now cold indifference. Each story we've looked at this week shows an opposite element to the blessing. We bless others when we have self-control, offer radical forgiveness like Christ urged Peter ("Not seven times . . . seventy times seven!"), point others to hope in Christ and the special future he offers, and express warmth through meaningful touch and verbalized praise and appreciation.

Circle which one of these four you most need God's help in living out today:

Self-control—Forgiveness—Hopefulness—Affection

Day 12

The senior photo—the one where you were younger, thinner, had hair.

The studio photo—it's amazing what a filter and an airbrush can do, isn't it?

The candid photo—hair's a mess, skin's blotchy, but, hey, get a load of that smile!

Okay, which of the three do you hang on the wall?

If it's a picture of me, I want the one with the best face, the one with the lighting that makes me look good, with the pose that stretches the sagging chin, with the color that highlights the eyes. Of course, if it's pictures of other people, then I want the candid ones because in a candid shot something of the personality comes out. An expression you get that you can't get in a studio. A spontaneity that somehow liberates the spirit. That's why I think we like them.

Do you create a setting in your home that encourages that kind of spontaneity? Do you try to capture a certain look, or do you catch what comes? And are you satisfied with what comes? Do the people in your life feel you're satisfied with what comes, even delighted with what comes? Or do they feel you're wanting picture-perfect relationships and that they don't have the right clothes or the right hair or the right whatever to pull that off?

When you finally have time to put all those photos in albums, it's the candid ones you'll enjoy most. Wild hair and all! So why not enjoy those moments now while the kids are still at home and you still have plenty of film!

Almighty God. Ruler. Creator. Sustainer. When it's you who holds the very stars in the sky, why do I want to control things so much? I know why, Lord. Sadly, it's because I often trust you so little and think far too much of myself. My way. My rights. My way of staging and shooting the picture so it looks just the way I want it. Help me to see that trying to be perfect or to look perfect is a slippery, unbiblical slope. Help me laugh and loosen my grip and allow those candid shots at times that can capture true joy.

Do you struggle with perfectionism? Does someone you live with? What role can high control, perfectionism, or fear of failure play in keeping us from living the blessing?

Day 13

Movies have had a powerful effect on our culture. A movie like *Saturday Night Fever* comes out, and the whole country goes disco. A movie like *Flashdance,* and the whole country is wearing torn sweatshirts. *Risky Business,* and everyone's buying the sunglasses Tom Cruise wore.

Movies affect us not only culturally but personally. The images flashed on movie screens are images we take with us when we leave the theater. They have a subliminal effect on us that is enormous. The images shape our understanding of how we should relate husband to wife, parent to child, friend to friend.

Take this image for example.

Marion doesn't seem a very manly name, but it was the name of the movie star who became an icon of manliness for millions. His full name was Marion Michael Morrison. His film name was John Wayne. The Duke.

The images he left behind on the screen impacted the male consciousness for over four decades. His pictures projected the image of a man who was his own man, a man nobody owned or ordered around. He pulled himself up by his bootstraps. He shot straight and rode tall. He went *his* way, on his own horse. And he was famous for lines like the one he delivered in the film *She Wore a Yellow Ribbon:* "Never apologize, mister. It's a sign of weakness."

It's not true, of course. But hearing the Duke say it and seeing him on the screen larger than life, it seems it should be true.

That is the power of a picture, especially the picture of someone we look up to. Even if what he or she says isn't true, it seems true to us because the person looms larger than life. That person may be a movie star, a coach, a teacher.

Or a father.

The following thoughts are from a man reflecting on the pictures he had left one day in his son's life. I think he's the type of man John Wayne would have wanted as a father . . . before he was the Duke and was just little Marion.

Listen son, I am saying this as you lie asleep, one little paw crumpled under your cheek and the blonde curls sticky wet on your forehead. Just a few moments ago, I sat, reading my paper in the library, and a stifling wave of remorse swept over me. Guiltily I came to your bedside.

These are the things I was thinking, son: I had been cross to you. I scolded you as you were crossing the street because you didn't look both ways before coming over to see me; I didn't like it, and told you so when you just gave your face a dab with the towel. I took you to task for not cleaning your shoes. I called angrily when you threw some of your things on the floor.

At breakfast I found fault, too. You spilled things. You gulped down your food. You put your elbows on the table. You spread butter too thick on your bread. And as you started off to play, and I made for my bus, you turned and waved a hand and called, "Goodbye, Daddy," and I frowned and said in reply, "Hold your shoulders back."

Then it began all over again in the late afternoon. As I came up the road I spied you, down on your knees, playing marbles. There were holes in your stockings. I humiliated you before your boy friends by marching you straight to the house ahead of me. Stockings were expensive—and if you had to buy them, you'd be more careful. . . .

Do you remember later, when I was reading in the library, how you came in timidly, with a sort of hurt look in your eyes? When I glanced up over my paper, impatient at the interruption, you hesitated at the door, and I snapped, "What do you want?"

You said nothing, just ran across in one tempestuous plunge, threw your arms around my neck and kissed me. And then you were gone, pattering up the stairs.

Well, son, it was shortly afterward that my paper slipped from my hands and a terrible sickening feeling came over me. What has habit been doing to me? The habit of finding fault, or reprimanding. . . . It was not that I didn't love you; it was that I expected too much of you. I was measuring you by the yardstick of my own years.

There's so much that is good and fine in your little character. It didn't matter what I said, you came in with a spontaneous burst of childish emotion, and rushed across the room to kiss me goodnight. Nothing else matters tonight, son. I have come to your bedside in the darkness, and I have knelt there, ashamed!. . . .

Tomorrow, son, I'll be a real daddy. I'll be kind and thoughtful. I'll laugh when you laugh, and cry when you cry. Don't worry about me, son. I'll remember how important you are, and I'll remember who you are.

I'm afraid I've visualized you as a man. Yet, as I look at you now, son, peacefully sleeping in your little bed, I see that you are still a baby. Yesterday you were in your mother's arms, your head on her shoulder. I have asked too much.

I have expected you to be a man, son, and you're only a little boy.

My little boy.

W. Livingston Larned, "A Father Forgets"

As you look at your little boy or girl—at your older brother or younger sister, at your arthritic mother or aging father, at your pastor or youth worker or school administrator or best friend—don't be afraid to apologize. Don't just rehearse it in your mind or confess it in your prayers by the bedside of the one you've hurt. Pick the right time to talk about it, but talk about it.

No matter what anybody tells you, apologizing isn't a sign of weakness. It's a sign of strength.

And it leaves behind a *great* picture!

Lord, I don't need to discuss anything after reading that father's story. I need to pray. For moments I could have blessed my child but didn't. For the angry words I've said or the kind words never spoken. And for the power, with your love and strength, to do better. Tonight. Tomorrow. Right now. Lord, let me muster up the courage, for it will take courage for me to fight back my pride and finally say, "All right, Paul . . . or Mary . . . I'm sorry."

Day 14

Recently Cindy and I were at a conference where we met little Aaron's mother. She came up quietly. Shared her story softly. And left a profound impact on our lives. That is, after we all stopped crying and thanking God for what he'd done.

It seems that when Aaron was only three, he developed viral meningitis. As a result of his sudden, uncontrollable fever, he lost his hearing. But he had a mom and dad who didn't see that as a barrier to giving him the blessing. To them it was just a small fence they had to step over.

To do that, they learned sign language so they could keep telling their son they loved him . . . and keep singing to him too.

And of all the published and polished songs they could have chosen to sing to him, they picked an unpublished, spur-of-the-moment-created, "good morning" song that Cindy and I had made up for our children. A blessing song that had ended up on a video we'd done a dozen years ago.

Aaron's parents saw the video and Cindy and me singing our little song to Kari and Laura, and they adopted it for their home. Every morning they sang Aaron the "blessing" song. And they kept on singing . . . using sign language . . . after he lost his hearing.

The song has simple words and a very simple melody. "Good morning, good morning, how are you today? The Lord bless you and keep you throughout the day. We love you, we love you, we love you, Kari . . . or Laura . . ." or in this case, Aaron.

I think of how many children I've met whose parents never bothered to call or come home or say "I love you" or write that letter of blessing which is so long overdue. Then I think of Aaron.

The wonderful news. Through the miracle of modern medicine and three high-tech operations, he has most of his hearing back today. But some things haven't changed. Like the way his parents still sing, "I love you . . . the Lord bless you . . ." to a young boy who has never once failed to hear those words.

I take so much for granted, Lord. My health. My children's health. Would I have the faith and determination of Aaron's parents to fight through the barriers and bless my children no matter what? I hope so. I pray so. Today.

Lord, I've let many things block me from being a person of blessing. We've looked at several this week, such as anger and bitterness and pride. Help me remember that you can knock down every barrier. Lord, there's this one barrier I'm still facing. I'll express it here. But I would ask you to blow it down and build something new and honoring to you in its place:

Bless, O Lord, My Family

Day 15

We've spent one week reviewing aspects of what it means to bless others and another looking at the barriers that keep us from doing so. Now it's time to take an extended look at where the blessing should begin. From Almighty God through his Son to our family first of all.

So let me begin by asking you a question.

Are you for real?

Do you accept with joy the words, "Hi, Grandma!" or do you bristle inside because "You're not that old."

Do you admit you have faults . . . even to your children? Or do you pick them to pieces without removing the log in your eye?

Edith Schaeffer has a story that speaks of being "real" in a family.

Memories not chosen, but given day by day, are also being collected. Is a slap in the face the first memory? Or is it the memory of Mommy still being there when the early streaks of dawn starting to come in through the curtains startle you into seeing that "Mommy has been up all night because I had the croup. She didn't go to bed at all. Oh, Mommy!" You can't choose the first memory; you can't regulate what will be remembered and what will be forgotten. If there are enough lovely memories, and if there are apologies for making really wrong choices, then the museum will have a good balance and a nonromantic reality of what life is like.

Of course, there will also be memories of flare-ups in the family. "Daddy is awfully mad right now!" can be said by a four-year-old without any tragic results. "Mommy is in a bad humor; I'm going to stay in here till she feels better!" will not harm any child. The reality of the ups and downs of dispositions, of people's tempers or of their mistakes and actual sins, does not tear apart the museum of memories, nor does it have to tear up the home or split the family. A realistic facing of the imperfections, faults, weaknesses, blind spots, and sins of each other in the family, although it will never be a complete facing of the whole person, will be a measure of understanding the whole person which will give a preparation for the future.

Edith Schaeffer, *What Is a Family?*

We could all use a little help when it comes to leaving behind pictures in people's lives, partly because much of the time we don't think anyone is focusing a camera on us. But of course they are. Other people are taking pictures all the time. When we first get up, someone's there watching. Before the shower, before the makeup, before the coffee. When we finally go to bed, someone's watching. After the makeup comes off, and the teeth or the toupee or anything else that isn't a real part of us. At work. Over coffee. On the court. At the mall. We're leaving pictures all over the place.

What parts of the pictures are real? Is it all just so much makeup, so much hair coloring, so much of so many things that make us appear to be something we're not?

Sometime or another, people are going to see us in our emotional underwear. They're going to see us tired, depressed, frustrated, angry, snippy, and selfish. The people we love need to see those pictures, too, so that when they say they love us, it's the *real* us they love, not some airbrushed image.

Thank you, Lord, that you are who you are. When asked your name, you said, "I am who I am." No image. No cover-up. No fakery or smoke and mirrors. Thank you, Lord Jesus, for being the way, the truth, and the life.

How difficult is it for you to be "real"—warts and all—with your loved ones? Would they say you're authentic and willingly admit your faults? Have you asked them?

Do you agree that in a family, being "real" is a very real part of giving the blessing? Why or why not?

Day 16

Edith Schaeffer also talks about the importance of choice when it comes to leaving pictures of blessing in the lives of those you love. Sit with her awhile, and make room in your heart for her words to live and grow and bear fruit.

> *How do you choose a memory? . . .*
>
> *You've gone to the doctor or the dentist or the grocery shopping or to do a business errand some distance from home. You are together as a whole family—or you and your husband are alone or with one child or a sister of yours or a friend. The "efficient" thing to do is to take the first bus or train or subway back home—but actually there is an hour or two or three that you could choose to use in a different way. You could take the boat back from Lausanne, if you live in that part of the world. It would take longer, but you would have a lifetime memory of the sunset on the lake, a cup of tea in the tearoom on the boat, the feeling of being far away from everything, although you are actually a very short distance from the train rushing along the shore of the lake.*
>
> *What you have taken is three hours to cover a distance you could have covered in about a fifth of the time, because of the schedules as well as the slower pace of the boat. Is it worth it? The same ticket is accepted on the boat as on the train.*
>
> *It is time we are talking about. Time not planned ahead, but*

decided upon on the spur of the moment. Shall we do this? Is it worth it to take two or three extra hours, when you could "get all that done at home" or "at the office"? Upon what basis is your decision? This is the crucial place of understanding where many people are blind. . . . Many times you are not choosing what to do with two or three hours for the immediate result, but you are choosing a memory (or choosing not to have that memory) for a lifetime. For years the ten-year-old and the three- and five-year-old will remember the bubbles of excitement that came when Mother and Daddy said, "We have finished the doctor's appointment and we could take the next tram [or drive home on the expressway as fast as possible], but we have decided to turn off and go to the zoo [or the aquarium or the birdhouse in the park]. We didn't plan to do this, but we thought it would be fun for all of us."

The bubble of excitement, the thrill that comes in being loved and considered important, the reality of discovering that our mother and father really like being together with us, the highlighted enjoyment of whatever it is you decide to do, will make it a stronger, longer-lasting and more vivid memory than even the planned days off could ever be. The memory multiplies the use of those hours into hundreds of hours!

Edith Schaeffer, *What Is a Family?*

If you make children happy now, you will make them happy twenty years hence by the memory of it.

Kate Douglas Wiggin

Loving Father, I'm in such a hurry so much of the time. On this day, filled with appointments—soccer practice or rushing

to do errands — let me capture a moment to create a memory,
for the gift of my time is a powerful tool for blessing.

What do I gain, *really*, by being so busy?

What have I gained recently by carving out a moment in my schedule to bless someone else?

Day 17

Memories are not years or days. Memories are moments.

Linda and Richard Eyre, Teaching Your Children Sensitivity

Norman Lear, producer of such television series as *All in the Family* and of such films as *Fried Green Tomatoes,* was asked to choose a single picture that moved him most and to explain why it moved him.

He chose a picture of a woman kneeling against a bed, her face even with the face of her baby, looking into the baby's eyes. Here is how he describes the photograph's impact:

This picture brought me to my knees. . . . I saw it for the first time in the fifties in the book The Family of Man. *. . .*

I felt a kind of ultimate sweetness. In fact, I can't imagine a sweeter moment, or a sweeter depiction of a moment. It is the moment of a mother's spiritual, emotional recognition of a child. I've always assumed the child's eyes are open as the moment's evolving. There's something so deep here. The umbilical connection is a look, and that look is so powerful. They are separate individuals, but they are so tied together, eye to eye. . . .

Moments like the one in this picture are there so rarely, but they

*are there far more than we're able to experience them. The great
challenge is to find a way to live in the moment and experience
more of them. . . .*

Norman Lear quoted in *Talking Pictures: People Speak About the Photographs That Speak to Them*
by Marvin Heiferman and Carole Kismaric

---

*Moses saw your face, Lord. Face to face. "As a man sees another
man." He saw you, Lord, in all your preincarnate glory. And
his face shown because of it. And Lord, you've put some of that
awesome glow in the eyes of a mother and her newborn baby.
Thank you.*

Drag out your baby pictures. The kids will love it as they laugh and
point. You'll be astounded by the love you see in your mother's eyes. That
is, if you can find a picture, usually the candid variety, of your mother looking at you. Right now, what is your last memory of your mother looking at
you? Was it warm with love and connection? Or a flash of anger or indifference?

What look did you last leave with your children?

Day 18

The classic writer Dostoyevsky said: "Every day and every hour, every minute,
walk around yourself and watch yourself, and see that your image be seemly.
You pass by a little child, you pass by, spiteful, with ugly words, with wrath-
ful heart; you may not have noticed the child, but he has seen you, and your
image, unseemly and impious, may remain in his defenseless heart. You don't
know it, but you may have sown an evil seed in him and it may grow, and all
because you were not careful before the child. . . ."

The contemporary writer Robert Fulghum said something similar, only more succinctly: "Don't worry that your children never listen to you; worry that they are always watching you."

Children perceive life in concrete terms rather than abstract. The younger the children are, the truer this is. That's why children's books start out as picture books instead of only text for the parent to read aloud.

As children grow older, words accompany the pictures in their books. As they reach adulthood, they are weaned to reading books that have all print and no pictures.

To younger children, the abstract concepts of the gospel—love, atonement, repentance, reconciliation—slip like SpagettiOs through the grasp of their tiny, mental fingers. For them, the abstractions become concrete as they observe your life.

What does a child see in the life you're living?

A child sees pictures. A few one day that a nephew sees—the way you look him in the eyes or the way you look past him. A few more the next day that a neighbor kid sees—a picture of you shoveling snow from their driveway or one of you just shoveling your own. And a few more a kid sees at some school sporting event—a picture of you encouraging the players or one of you chewing out the ref.

What snapshots are they picking up? Snapshots that incarnate love or hate or merely indifference? Ones that say "Play fair," or "Do whatever it takes to win"? Ones that say "Get out of my way," or "Here, let me help you with that"?

They're listening to you. Whether they're your children or someone else's, they're listening. But more than listening, they're watching.

For the sake of the least of these, be careful what pictures you are leaving in their impressionable hearts. For as Jesus warned, it would be better that a millstone be tied around our necks and we be thrown into the sea than for us to cause even one of these little children to stumble.

Lord, you left us so many pictures. The ones of a Good
Samaritan and a Good Shepherd. A grain of wheat and a

house built on sand. Especially pictures of you on the cross.
Before we knew there were words like omniscience and
omnipresence to describe you, we had pictures. Such as when
you calmed the sea and made the blind to see or the dead to
rise. Thank you for those big pictures of your love.

Think about three areas of your life that one day your children will handle themselves. Finances. Free time. Study times. What pictures are you leaving now that will make your children better stewards? Better able to find genuine rest? Better equipped to go deep into God's Word? Do any of those pictures need to change?

Day 19

The names are changed and some of the scenes, but by and large what follows is a true story. It's the story of a father who died too soon to leave behind many memories. This is one he did leave. It was captured in the eyes and developed in the heart of the son who loved him.

The best thing that happened that day was the second time Teddy
and his father went swimming. . . .
    Mr. Schroeder told Teddy that now he had learned how to ride
the waves, he was ready to swim out to the barrels. The barrels were
quite a way from shore and had been anchored there to show that it
wasn't safe to swim any farther. Only the stronger, more experienced
swimmers went that far usually, and there were ropes tied between
the barrels so there would be something for them to hang on to when
they did. Mr. Schroeder said that he and Teddy would just take it
easy and everything would be fine.

About half way there they came upon Grandma Schroeder swimming a little distance away. She was so fat that you might have thought she couldn't swim at all but you would have been wrong. She was so fat that she floated like a cork, and Mrs. Schroeder said it would take a torpedo to sink her. There she was bobbing around in the ocean with her white bathing cap strapped under her chin and her cheeks bulging out of it. She could hardly believe her eyes when she saw Teddy dog-paddling along beside his father. She waved at him and he waved back at her, and he was proud that she had seen him out so far and doing the kind of thing that she thought boys were supposed to do for a change.

She didn't look to him as if she could ever be cross. She didn't look as if she would ever say a mean thing to Grandpa about drinking too many highballs or about how if it wasn't for her father they'd all be in the poorhouse. She didn't look rich or fierce. She just looked as if she was having a good time. She looked jolly and friendly and almost young with her bathing cap bouncing up and down in the sun like a balloon.

But the best part of the day happened just a little while afterward. Teddy thought the barrels still looked a long way off, and the beach was so far behind he could hardly recognize his mother and Bean sitting on it. His arms were beginning to ache, and he was feeling out of breath. What if he started to drown, he thought. What if he called for help and his father, who was a little ahead of him, didn't hear? What if a giant octopus swam up from below and wrapped him in its slimy green tentacles?

But just as he was thinking these things, his father turned around and treaded water, waiting for him.

"How about a lift the rest of the way?" Mr. Schroeder said. So Teddy paddled over and put his arms around his father's neck from behind, and that was the best part of the day for him and the part he remembered for many years afterward.

He remembered how the sunlight flashed off his father's freckly, wet shoulders and the feel of the muscles working inside them as he swam. He remembered the back of his father's head and the way his ears looked from behind and the way his hair stuck out over them. He remembered how his father's hair felt thick and wiry like a horse's mane against his cheek and how he tried not to hold on to his neck too tightly for fear he'd choke him.

His mother said bad things about his father. She said that he had no get-up-and-go and that he was worse than Grandpa Schroeder already although thirty years younger. She said that he needed a swift kick in the pants and things like that. And Teddy knew that his father did things that he wished he wouldn't, like drink too many cocktails and drive his car up on the lawn and come to kiss him and Bean goodnight with his face all clammy and cold.

But as he swam out toward the barrels on his father's back, he also knew that there was no place in the whole Atlantic Ocean where he felt so safe.

Frederick Buechner, The Wizard's Tide

Who knows what our children will remember, what moments in their past will be freighted with significance? Who knows what all they will see or when they will see it or how they will look back on it years from now when we're gone?

We can't know. None of us can know.

But we *can* love. Knowing that love makes the best pictures, we can love well and love often, increasing the chances that at whatever moment the shutter clicks, the picture will be looked back on the way Teddy looked back on his.

We need pictures like that as we dog-paddle our way through the vast and uncertain ocean that is life. Pictures that make us feel safe.

Safe in the eyes that look back for us.

Safe in the face that smiles at us.

Safe in the voice that calls to us—"How about a lift the rest of the way?"

Our Rock and our Hiding Place, thank you, Lord, that while
the safest place in all the Atlantic might be a father's shoulders,
the safest place in all the universe is in our Father's arms. You
guard us. Protect us. Sustain us. Thank you for being our
Good Shepherd in these dark, scary times.

Can you remember a time with your parents when you felt safe and especially loved? A special moment when they hugged away a fear or helped you through a trial? Write about it here or tell someone how they blessed you.

Are you providing that type of safety and security in your home today? What could you do to make it more secure or stable?

Day 20

Slowing down. Looking eye to eye. Living our authenticity. Providing a place of safety. All those things are wonderful ways of attaching high value to—blessing—our family. Yet here's something often overlooked that can leave its mark of "high value" as well.

Children are very sensitive to their parents' reasons for doing
something with or for them. Do parents think they ought to do this,
or do they really enjoy it? Is Mother reading a story because she
wants to quiet me down? Or is it because she thinks it's her duty?
Perhaps she thinks I'll enjoy this particular story, or being read to by
her, or both? Obviously it is a more rewarding experience for a child
if he can sense his mother's desire to give him pleasure.

Bruno Bettelheim, "Exploring Childhood as an Adult"

One of my favorite memories involves just such a time of sharing a
book. Traveling abroad we had purchased Elizabeth Goudge's

The Little White Horse *for our twelve-year-old son to read. He enjoyed it so much he repeatedly said, "Mom, you've just got to read this book." One night I stayed back from an art lecture in Florence, Italy, which I had hoped to attend and spent the evening with him instead. I read that book. I was as delighted as he, and commented on the incidents as I read. He was absorbed in his own book, but suddenly came over to my chair, gave me a tight hug, and said spontaneously, "I just had to tell you this minute I loved you!" I was taking time to enjoy his book. I treasure that evening. No art lecture could have done for us what sharing that book did. . . .*

Gladys Hunt, *Honey for a Child's Heart*

We value other people—whether children or coworkers—by taking delight in what they delight in. Genuine delight, not feigned. Those at work can see through pictures like that. So can those at play.

Take the time to create a picture for someone you love.

Humble yourself to enter his or her world. And when you cross that threshold, leave your own world behind. Open your heart to the things that give the other person delight, and see if there isn't something that delights you as well.

Remember what it was like to delight in something. Remember what it was like to skip and to hum and to laugh so hard you rolled on the floor, holding your sides because they ached so much.

What I'm saying is, become a child again.

Who knows what wonderful worlds will open. Who knows what wonderful things you will see. And who knows who may suddenly come over to your chair, give you a tight hug, and say, "I just had to tell you this moment I loved you!"

Looking at how you humbled yourself to be born in a stable, it shames me that I have such a hard time humbling myself to play dolls or Guess Who or Checkers or even Beanie Babies. My children want me to enter their world. And their joy when I stop

and stoop down to play is a tiny picture of the indescribable joy I
feel in knowing you humbled yourself to become a man.

Is it difficult for you to get down on your children's level? Or spend time with them watching their sport? Or going to their favorite Christian artist's concert? What keeps you from humbling yourself and entering their world?

Day 21

Pictures of blessing.

They come from imperfect people, insensitive people, impatient people. People like you and me.

They come not simply from those of us who've blown it but also from those of us who know we've blown it. From those of us who get on our knees and ask for grace to keep from blowing it again.

Marjorie Holmes was such a person. So many of her books are books of prayers that ask for forgiveness for her mistakes and for the grace to keep from making those mistakes again. Because she kept on her knees, she kept giving pictures of blessing to those she loved.

That's where pictures of blessing start to be developed. On our knees.

Take a minute to pray through one of Marjorie's prayers, pausing here and there to personalize it, thinking about specific things in your relationship with your own children.

Please teach me to talk to my children. With patience, good humor,
sympathy and understanding (insofar as it is possible for an adult to
understand his children).

And teach me to listen to them in a way that will make them
want to talk to me.

I am so often baffled by the things they say, shocked by the expressions they use. It sometimes upsets me to know they have the ideas they express.

Then I realize that this is the only way we can hope to bridge the differences between our generations. This frank, free exchange of thoughts.

Help me to keep my emotions out of it, Lord.

Don't let me get my feelings hurt; don't let me get mad. Keep me from sentimental comparisons (how much harder we had things at their age, how respectful and considerate we were to our parents). Guard me against faultfinding and accusations of ungratefulness.

O, God, teach me to talk to my children with tact and common sense.

Let me be open to their arguments; don't let me pretend to know all the answers. Let me be honest with them. Don't let me compromise my values. Don't let me be arrogant either. Don't let a desire to be right dominate my desire for genuine communication.

Let love, genuine love, pervade our conversations. Let laughter give it joy and flavor.

Lord, teach me to talk, and to listen, to my children so that they will always want to come back.

Marjorie Holmes, "Teach Me to Talk to Them"

Forgive me, Lord, for always going to you with my needs but so often failing to have a listening ear for my loved ones. I just assume you'll be there. That you want to know my needs and hurts, my goals and dreams. I should know that's what my children want too. For children love to talk to their parents, like I love to talk to you. Thank you, Lord, for always, always listening. Make that a trait they see in my life, I pray.

Why is it so hard to listen? The book of Proverbs teaches, "He who speaks before he hears, it is counted as foolishness to him." We're foolish when we speak before we listen. Unfortunately, I'm foolish too much of the time. How about you?

On a 1 to 10 scale, where 10 is "awesome listener" and "1" is "What did you say?" or worse, where would you rate with your spouse? With your children? With those who come to you for advice or counsel? Would you bless others more by listening more?

Day 22

I remember with special fondness the English teacher in my high school who sat on the corner of her desk and enchanted us with the music of Sir Walter Scott's Lady of the Lake:

> *The stag at eve had drunk its fill,*
> *Where danced the moon on Monan's rill,*
> *And deep his midnight lair had made*
> *In lone Glenartney's hazel shade. . . .*

Later, as a teacher myself, I knew the delight of taking children into a great adventure with a story—the utter silence of the room, the intent look on the children's faces, and the involuntary sigh that escaped our lips at the conclusion of the episode. We had been together in the presence of good writing, and we felt bound together by the experience. My sojourn in that school was brief, but only recently a former student met me unexpectedly and eagerly told me what book she was reading. She could have paid me no greater compliment.

Gladys Hunt, Honey for a Child's Heart

The teacher who read to little Gladys Hunt communicated more than a story when she read. With her inflections, her pauses, her diction she communicated that their imaginations were important, that their pleasure was important, that *they* were important.

Reading to children—whether they're your children or your grandchildren, your students or the kids in your carpool—leaves behind some great pictures.

Something is made visible when you read the words of a story. When the child hears the delight in your voice, sees the excitement in your eyes, and feels the drama in your pauses, something inside you is made tangible to the child and taken into the child's heart. When you and your mate are in bed at night and one of you is reading to the other, something of one person's heart is passed to the heart of the other. When you are on a long trip with a friend and the one who's not driving reads a book out loud, pausing here and there to comment or to ask a question or to discuss what's been read, something of that person's inner self has been revealed to the other person, offered to the other person, and received by the other person.

Through the earthly elements of ink and the thin white pages of a book, something of one soul is passed to another

Almost like a sacrament.

Lord, without a doubt, reading your Word is one of the greatest gifts we've been blessed with. From the patriarchs and the prophets to Palm Sunday and Pentecost, history is indeed your story. May my love for reading, and reading your Word, be a blessing I pass down to my children.

It's such a simple thing, reading with your children, but it can combine every element of the parental blessing. Meaningful touch as we sit next to them or with them in our laps. Spoken words where we make them the hero or heroine, high value shown in the time we spend, and a special future in our wish for more times like that.

How about reading a favorite story to your child—even if it's over the phone or on a family gathering when they're grown. It can bring back wonderful memories and another opportunity to share the blessing.

Day 23

There's a wonderful, true story of a man who left behind an unforgettable picture for his wife and kids, who were leaving for a family vacation. They were leaving without him because he had to stay behind and work, but he helped them plan in meticulous detail every day of the camping trip. The trip was to start at their home in Montgomery, Alabama. They were to drive to California, travel up and down the West Coast, and then make their way back to Montgomery.

Knowing their entire route, their camping sites, and their times of arrival, he pinpointed the precise time they would be crossing the Great Divide. Then he arranged to fly to the nearest airport and took a cab to take him to the place on the highway where every car had to pass. Once there, he sat by the roadside for several hours, waiting for their station wagon to come into sight. When it did, he stepped onto the road and put his thumb out to hitchhike a ride.

The family, as you could well imagine, got the surprise of their life when they saw him there, waiting for them. Imagine the laughter. Imagine the conversations. Imagine the memories.

A friend asked him why he went to all that trouble. "Well," he replied, "someday I'm going to be dead and when that happens I want my kids and my wife to say, 'You know, Dad was a lot of fun.'"

Bruce Larson, *The One and Only You*

Thank you, Lord, that each day is new. In fact you tell us,
"Thy mercies are new every morning. Great is thy
faithfulness." You also tell us that "in your presence is fullness of
joy." Newness of life. Fullness of joy. Thank you for your
creativity and deep, abiding joy that blesses our lives.

But, you're thinking, *I'm just not funny or spontaneous.* Try *planned spontaneity.* Often our lives are so busy we don't have time even to think about leaving or giving a blessing. So what's wrong with "scheduling" a time of affirmation? Plan a surprise party for your spouse, not a birthday or anniversary party, just an "I love you . . . and look at all these other people who do too" party. Or a "spontaneous" breakfast with each child . . . planned and noted on your calendar two weeks before. A time to tell them verbally that you love and bless them. Schedule in a time of closeness this week.

My commitment to schedule a time of closeness and blessing is for: _____.

When will it be?

Day 24

How do you know an object is symbolic? Because it initiates a string
of associations that can get you talking for hours. White gloves are
that way for me, but so are baseball gloves, like the one I once got as
a birthday present. I have a vivid picture of this glove sitting on the
dining room buffet right next to the fold-up cot I used to sleep in.
It's night in the memory, and I'm in bed, and our family is about to
go on vacation the next day. I can smell the neat's-foot oil that I've
rubbed into the glove, and I can see it glisten in the rays of a
streetlight outside the window. I know the memory isn't accurate
because my birthday is in early April and our family never went on

*vacation until school was out, late June at the earliest. But accuracy
doesn't matter. The memory fuses the best of April with the best of
June, and once I start talking about the glove, it brings back images
of playing catch with my father, of watching him play on his
softball team, and of doing the same things with my sons.*

John Kotre, *White Gloves: How We Create Ourselves Through Memory*

Memories are often passed from one generation to the next in the form of symbols, for example, a baseball glove. These symbols are an important part of a person's emotional vocabulary. They mean something, they say something. In the language of the heart, a baseball glove means "I want to spend time with you, have a relationship with you, be a part of your life, play catch."

I've played a lot of catch myself over the years. I was catcher on my junior high and high school teams. But I never had a catch with my dad. I think that's why the ending of the movie *Field of Dreams* touched me so deeply. Remember the final scene, the final words between Ray and his father?

"Hey . . . Dad . . . wanna have a catch?"

"I'd like that."

And as the two of them did, the years of absence began to be bridged . . . with the arc of baseball. So what is there to learn from a scene like that in a movie?

Play those games of catch. Or those games of Scrabble. Or dolls. Or whatever games your family plays. Play them while you can . . . so that someday when you can't, there will at least be the memories of when you could and did.

---

*Lord, there is someone I wish I could see again. Even if it were
for just a few moments. To say, "I'm sorry." "Let's try again." "I
forgive you." "I love you." If I don't get that chance this side of
heaven, thank you, Lord, that I can leave that "open loop"
with you. That you can provide closure for my heart, so I am
free to move forward from the past and bless my family today.*

In a family it helps so much to "close the loop." Are there conversations or actions with your parents or children that are still "open loops"? Unfinished conversations? Unspoken apologies? An unwillingness to make up or move on? What a blessing it would be to the rest of the family for you to be strong enough to initiate the peace.

Day 25

Charles Schultz, the cartoonist who created Charlie Brown, Lucy, and all the other characters in the *Peanuts* comic strip, had one picture that was forever etched in his memory. A picture of his grandmother. And the picture itself was filled with symbolism.

Her children all called her Ma. I called her Gramma. She had nine children and outlived six of them. To me, she was always old, and now I am older than she was when I thought she was old. For the last half of her life she depended completely on her children for support. While she lived mainly with us in Minnesota, she occasionally would take the train out to California and live for several months with another daughter until she missed my mother and returned to us.

Her photograph represents to me a portion of my life that was so significant it colored all the years that followed. . . .

The lines in her face represent all the tragedies in her life. She lost her husband when she was in her early thirties, and saw six of her children grow to adulthood, then die of diseases that could probably be cured easily today. Her photo casts images for me of the many hours she spent entertaining me by playing school. I was the teacher and she was the pupil. I gave her spelling tests and, because she had gone no further than third grade, she always misspelled at least a few of the words. She would go down into our basement with me and be the hockey goalie armed with a broom, while I shot tennis balls at her.

Now she is gone. My father and mother are gone. My father's barber shop is now someone's bar and grill, and my uncle who took the photograph and shared Army talk with me—we were both machine gunners—is gone. Most of my family photographs lie jumbled in a couple of boxes. Pictures of my own children are mixed in with pictures of my parents when they were young, but this photo of Gramma was placed in a small frame. I don't know when Gramma died, or where in California she was living when she died, and I don't know where she is buried, but my memory of her and that period in our lives is as vivid as this photo.

Charles Schultz, quoted in *Talking Pictures: People Speak About the Photographs*

That Speak to Them by Marvin Heiferman and Carole Kismaric

Thank you, Lord Jesus, for grandmas. Whether they had deep lines of faith and love or looked half their age, there is so much in grandmothers' unconditional love that reflects your own love. Help me to honor them—or their memory—by seeking to live out their love.

Stroll down memory lane to many families' "designated blesser." It's Grandma—including my grandmother, and I hope yours as well. Share a memory about her, about the blessing she left in your life. Remember the words of Christ's beloved disciple, "I have no greater joy than to know that my children walk in the light." Living a Christlike life honors a grandparent, as well as ourselves and our parents.

Bless, O Lord, the Way I Live My Life

Day 26

Washington, D.C., Memorial Day, 1986.

At one o'clock in the afternoon the ceremony to dedicate the Vietnam Veteran's Memorial began. Thousands had gathered for the dedication, some in coats and ties, some in faded army fatigues. Women and children had gathered there too.

The mood grew solemn as the master of ceremonies introduced the chairman of the memorial fund, who talked about healing the wounds caused by the bitter controversy over the war. After him a priest who had seen combat prayed and spoke of his feelings about the war.

When the program was over, a man and woman walked slowly along the memorial wall, their ten-year-old son trailing behind. The boy watched as people left things beside the wall. He trailed farther behind, looking at each plaque, studying each medal, examining every token of remembrance that had been left. Just before he ran to catch up with his parents, he took something out of his pocket and placed it beneath one of the panels on the wall.

It was a small blue marble.

It was all he had to give. It wasn't much. But it was his. He had taken it in his pocket all the way to Washington, D.C., and had left it as a memorial. Who knows why?

Maybe for no other reason than he had seen other people taking things out of their pockets and leaving them there.

Maybe it's the pictures we have seen somewhere in our past that touch the ten-year-old in all of us. And maybe that is why we dig into our pockets to leave something behind in other people's lives.

Even if it is just a small blue marble.

Almighty God, you created oceans and mountains and storms . . . and small boys with small blue marbles. Thank you, Lord, that even small acts of love or remembrance aren't discarded or forgotten in heaven. Help me to look for those small kindnesses someone has done for me this day and thank them.

As you continue to make living the blessing a conscious, daily decision, I'd encourage you to do two things.

First, think or perhaps read about someone whose life of service to God has been an inspiration to you. (Need help? How about reading Corrie Ten Boom's *The Hiding Place* or Jim Elliot's story *Through Gates of Splendor* or listening to Focus on the Family's cassette tape of the life of Dietrich Bonhoeffer). Ten-year-olds learn by watching. So do we.

Ask yourself, what is something from another's life of faith that I need to emulate?

Second, pick out a small gift, for instance, a flower, a postcard, a single wrapped chocolate. Place that small treasure in the hand of someone who needs help today looking up at the one who loves him or her so much.

Day 27

Every picture has a voice. Some have volume switches you can adjust, like the images that parade across your television screen day in and day out. Some scream at you with the hurricane force of multiple speakers and digital sound at the multiplex movie theater

in the mall. But still photographs talk, too. They grab our
attention and challenge us by saying, "Look at me. Buy me.
Remember me. Be like me." If every photograph has a job, it is to
say something.

Marvin Heiferman and Carole Kismaric

Talking Pictures: People Speak About the Photographs That Speak to Them

Every picture has a voice. Every photograph says something.

How about the picture people have of you? The picture in the billfold of the person at work. The picture framed in the hallway at home. The picture in the high school yearbook.

If you were to die today, what caption would the people who knew you put beneath your picture? What caption would your mother put? Your father? What caption would your mate put? Or your roommate? How about your closest friend? Your children? Your neighbor?

Take a minute to think of the word or phrase or Bible verse that summarizes how you would like to be remembered.

Do the pictures in their mind match the caption in yours?

Dear Lord, the idea that pictures "talk" scares me. I want them
to stop, to stay tame and safe behind the gloss and the white
border. But they do talk. And I pray that whether it's pictures
on the refrigerator or in someone's wallet or hanging in a
hallway, those pictures speak of your love, seen through the
blessing I gave them.

It's hard to imagine a time when there weren't "talking pictures." But there was, only that was "way back then." Now, we're stuck . . . or blessed . . . with "talkies." One way to get your family "talking" is to have everyone sit around the kitchen table and create a "family coat of arms," a shield, with four sections. And each person draws or writes down four things that represent your family. Get ready for a great discussion!

Day 28

*One woman had [a vivid picture] of her mother the day her baby
was born. "I remember taking him to my mom—my mom had not
seen him—and I'll never forget the look. It, she, just crushed me.
She looked at him as if to say, 'Is that him?'" This woman knew
that there was far more to this memory than the moment it
captured. Her mother's look was the one she had always received as
a child, her mother's attitude the one that had always met the things
she produced. Nothing, in fact, could serve as a better metaphor for
the extended nature of this mother-daughter relationship than the
memory of that glance.*

John Kotre, *White Gloves: How We Create Ourselves Through Memory*

That glance. How many of us have seen it sometime in our lives? How
often has the flashbulb gone off when such a glance was given? And how long
has the picture remained in our memories? Can you see it now?

The raising of an eyebrow.

The squinting of an eye.

A closing of the eyelids.

A flutter of the lashes.

The wrinkling of a forehead.

A pursing of the lips.

The shaking of a head.

The cocking of a neck.

The clucking of a tongue.

The gaping of a mouth.

That glance is captured in a fraction of a second. The picture of that
glance is endured for a lifetime.

Or enjoyed for a lifetime, depending on the glance.

So practice your glances. Try saying something kind with your eyes and
something nice with your face. The glimmer in the eye that says "I'm so

proud of you." The smiling glance that says "You're special." The adoring gaze that says "I love you more than words can ever express."

If people take pictures of something as slight as a glance, make sure the one they take of you gets framed on the walls of their hearts, not shoved in some bottom drawer.

I'm glad I wasn't Peter when he caught your glance, Lord Jesus, after he denied you three times. But in many ways, I've seen it too. When I've fallen. And failed. And sometimes I didn't even care. But a single glance from you can bring not only conviction but new life, like you gave the thief on the cross. Thank you, Lord, for looking my way.

Finally! One element of the blessing you don't have to work or worry about! You're not giving anyone "dirty looks" or glances! Wait a minute . . . *are you sure?* Wouldn't this be a good time to say, without advance preparation, "Honey, as best you can, show me how I look when I'm upset with you or with the kids"? It might shock you to see that living mirror . . . or give you another goal to bless and add, not curse and take away.

Day 29

Remember Gerald Sittser's story? His wife, Lynda, his daughter, Diana Jane, and his mother were all killed in a collision with a drunk driver. In a terrifying instant they were torn from his life. Here's what remained.

I have photographs of Lynda, Diana Jane, and my mother on the mantel in our living room. I still have not gotten used to seeing them there. I gaze at the photographs of people I once knew and enjoyed, lived with, talked to, and held in my arms. Their pictures fall far short of what they were in real life and what real life was with them. Immobile and lifeless, they are beautiful but dead, mere snapshots of people whom I knew as living people in the motion picture of our life together.

For the rest of his life Gerald would have only a mantel full of memories to look back on. Here, in his own words, are a few of his memories of Lynda.

Lynda was an unusual woman. She was gracious and energetic, simple, competent, and hospitable. She found joy in serving others, and she loved her children with all her heart. She worked hard from morning to evening, laughed far more than she cried, and delighted in ordinary life. She was good and guileless at the core of her being. I miss her as she was, not as I wished her to be. I lost a friend, a lover, a partner. Our life had found a rhythm of its own. Nearly every night, for example, we took a break around 10:00 P.M. In the summer we sat on the porch swing and drank a soda, and in the winter we sat on the living-room sofa and drank hot chocolate. We talked about the day, discussed how the children were doing, debated issues, told stories, laughed, and cuddled. Then we prayed together. We also enjoyed common interests like camping and backpacking, reading, music, gardening, and canning fruits and vegetables. We went out on dates together biweekly. We were partners in managing our home and raising the children. Our relationship was delightfully multi-dimensional. Her absence touches almost every area of my life.

Look back at the pictures Lynda left behind. Not the ones on the mantel. The ones in Gerald's life. Visualize them, one by one. And one by one, hear what they say.

I love you. I love our kids. I love the time we spend together, from the sodas to the stories and everything in between. I love our home, all the way down to the roots of the things that grow in its garden. I love it all. I love *you* all.

Through the pictures Lynda speaks. To her husband. To her children. To her friends. To everyone who knew her and loved her. And though her absence touches everything, so do the pictures she left behind.

Heavenly Father, I can't imagine the pain of losing a wife, and a daughter, and a mother, all at the same terrible moment. But while not so quickly, nor with so many at once, I've had my share of losses. And you've always been faithful. Always been there. Always been the truest source of comfort. Thank you that you made tear ducts and in your Word even mandated time for grieving. And especially, thanks for turning ashes to beauty and sorrow to song.

Who is someone you've lost that was very important in your life? That person's life can still be a blessing as you remember and honor the memory. Why not share with a spouse or close friend a bit of how that special someone blessed you.

Day 30

The following is the prayer of a teenage boy.

DID YOU EVER FAIL, LORD?

*No one pays any attention to me
or what I say, Lord.
I'm nobody, I guess.
I haven't done anything important
or made anything*

or won anything.
No one listens when I talk;
no one asks my opinion.
I'm just there
like a window
or a chair.

I tried to build a boat once,
but it fell apart.
I tried to make the baseball team,
but I always threw past third base.
I wrote some articles
for our school paper,
but they didn't want them.
I even tried out for the school play,
but the other kids laughed
when I read my lines.
I seem to fail
at everything.

I don't try anymore
because I'm afraid to fail.
And no one likes to fail
all the time.

If only there was something I could do,
something I could shout about,
something I could make
that was my work,
only mine.
And people would say,
"David did that!"
And my parents would say,
"We're proud of you, son!"
But I can't do anything.

Everyone else is so much better
at everything
than I am.
The more I fail
the more it eats away at me
until I feel weak inside.
I feel like I'm nothing.

Lord,
the world seems full of heroes
and idols and important people.

Where are all the failures?
Where are they hiding?
Where are people like me?
Did you ever fail, Lord?
Did you?
Do you know how I feel?
Do you know what it's like
when everyone looks up at you and says:
"He's a failure."

David

Norman Habel, *For Mature Eyes Only*

Sad, isn't it? More than sad, it's tragic the pictures this teenager has carried for so long in his billfold. Take a minute to look at them, won't you?

A boat that fell apart.

Can you see the hopeful white of the Polaroid starting to develop,
then slowly turning dark, him alone in his garage, pounding away with
a hammer, getting more and more frustrated as a nail bends or the sail breaks?

Baseball tryouts where he made a fool of himself.

The coach dismissing him with a shake of his head. The more athletic
boys clumped together, whispering, pointing, snickering.

Getting the article back from the editor of the school newspaper.

The look of disappointment in his eyes. The flush of embarrassment over his face.

Tryouts for the school play.

David is waiting his turn, measuring himself against all who went before him, trying to remember his lines, stomach churning as he tucks in his shirt, cinches his belt. It's his turn now, and when he delivers his lines, his voice cracks. On her clipboard the instructor takes note. So does everyone else.

Do you see what's happening?

David is dying, a picture at a time.

Maybe he's someone you know or someone you barely know. Maybe he's the kid next door or your own kid. Maybe he's grown now, and he's an uncle or someone you work with. There's someone like David in all of our lives. And he desperately needs a new set of pictures to live by.

Take a moment to think who that is in your life. When you see that person in your mind, think about him or her or them. Think about who they are, what they've been through, how they feel about themselves. Then think of a picture you can leave behind, a picture that says "David did that!" or "I'm proud of you!"

The pictures you leave in his life may be the ones that someday keep him, in a moment of despair, from taking his life.

The gospel. It's about all the Davids of this world and the Emilys and the old Mr. What's-His-Names . . . and giving them a new set of pictures to live by.

Oh, gracious Heavenly Father. Thank you so much that you were there every time I felt so alone. That you are there when I fail and during those times I feel so . . . ordinary. Thank you for standing closer than my shadow and caring far more than anyone else ever could.

Today I prayed for _____—someone who I know has failed at something small or large and who I've tried to bless.

Day 31

This is the final day of our time together. We have talked and thought and prayed about a lot of important things about life in general and your life in particular. The following quote is from the introduction to *The Sacred Journey*, an autobiographical work about Frederick Buechner's childhood. Take a few minutes after you've read what he has written about his own life and spend those minutes reflecting on your own.

> *What I propose to do now is to try listening to my life as a whole, or at least to certain key moments of the first half of my life thus far, for whatever the meaning, of holiness, of God, there may be in it to hear. My assumption is that the story of any one of us is in some measure the story of all of us.*
>
> *For the reader, I suppose, it is like looking through someone else's photograph album. What holds you, if nothing else, is the possibility that somewhere among all those shots of people you never knew and places you never saw, you may come across something or someone you recognize. In fact—for more curious things have happened—even in a stranger's album, there is always the possibility that as the pages flip by, on one of them you may even catch a glimpse of yourself. Even if both of those fail, there is still a third possibility which is perhaps the happiest of them all, and that is that once I have put away my album for good, you may in the privacy of the heart take out the album of your own life and search it for the people and places you have loved and learned from yourself, and for those moments in the past—many of them half forgotten—through which you glimpsed, however dimly and fleetingly, the sacredness of your own journey.*

Frederick Buechner, The Sacred Journey

Thank you for taking the time to read my book
and for spending the last month thinking and praying
about the pictures you are leaving behind in other people's lives.
I pray that the pictures are a blessing.
That they are remembered.
And treasured.
And that someday, in some way,
they are passed on
to bless others.

If you'd like to pass on a picture of a blessing you've experienced,
I'd love to hear about it. Either a blessing you received or,
by God's grace, passed on.
I can promise I'll read every letter, even if I'm not able to send a response.
May the Lord bless and keep you.

John Trent

Notes

Chapter 1: To Be a Person of Blessing

1. The account of this story and others that surrounded the Oklahoma City bombing can be found in the book *Where Was God at 9:02 A.M.?*, by Robin Jones (Nashville: Nelson, 1995).

Chapter 3: Out of Control

1. Frederick Buechner, *Telling Secrets* (San Francisco: HarperSanFrancisco, 1991), 8-9,10.

Chapter 4: Jesus All Along

1. Gerald L. Sittser, *A Grace Disguised: How the Soul Grows Through Loss* (Grand Rapids: Zondervan, 1996), 50.

Chapter 5: Choosing to Change

1. Daniel Taylor, *The Healing Power of Stories* (New York: Doubleday, 1996), 1-2.

Chapter 6: Switching Fathers

1. Baal was the chief god in the pantheon of Canaanite deities. The word literally means "master" or "lord." They believed he ruled over some seventy lesser gods, and he was worshiped for his bestowal of fertility for all life—human, animal, and vegetable.

2. Asherah was a goddess in Canaanite mythology that was associated with Baal. Wooden objects called *asherim* (plural of *asherah*) were often carved and put in places of worship to honor the goddess.

3. Leon Wood, *A Survey of Israel's History* (Grand Rapids: Zondervan, 1970), 366.

Chapter 7: Responding to the Pain

1. Henry Orenstein, *I Shall Live* (New York: Simon & Schuster, 1987), xiii.

2. Nancy Churnin, "A Real 'Shayna Maidel' Helps Actress," *Los Angeles Times*, 6 April 1991, sec. F-16.

Chapter 8: An Embrace Where Choices Meet

1. The photograph, taken by Nick Ut, can be seen in the book *Talking Pictures: People Speak About the Photographs That Speak to Them*, by Marvin Heiferman and Carole Kismaric (San Francisco: Chronicle Books, 1994), 61.

2. The story behind the photograph has been adapted from *Seventy Times Seven*, by Johann Christoph Arnold (Farmington, Pa.: Plough House Publishing, 1997), 126-9.

Chapter 9: Healing for Going Forward

1. Sittser, *A Grace Disguised*, 81.

2. Sittser, *A Grace Disguised*, 85.

3. Lewis B. Smedes, *Forgive & Forget: Healing the Hurts We Don't Deserve* (New York: Simon & Schuster, 1984), 33-4.

Chapter 10: The Unfinished Business of the Past

1. Frederick Buechner, *A Room Called Remember* (San Francisco: Harper & Row, 1984), 4.

2. Larry Crabb, *Inside Out* (Colorado Springs: NavPress, 1988), 176.

3. Elie Wiesel, *From the Kingdom of Memory* (New York: Summit Books, 1990), 200-1.

4. Sittser, *A Grace Disguised*, 17-8.

5. Sittser, *A Grace Disguised*, 130.

6. Smedes, *Forgive & Forget*, 173.

7. Sittser, *A Grace Disguised*, 104-5.

8. Wayne Muller, *Legacy of the Heart: The Spiritual Advantages of a Painful Childhood* (New York: Simon & Schuster, 1992), 179.

9. Sittser, *A Grace Disguised*, 64.

10. Smedes, *Forgive & Forget*, 170.

Chapter 11: The Beginning of the End Is Remembrance

1. Brent Ashabranner, *Always to Remember: The Story of the Vietnam Veterans' Memorial* (New York: Scholastic, 1988), 66,69.

Chapter 13: The Horrible, Beautiful Picture

1. Joseph LeDoux, *The Emotional Brain* (New York: Simon & Schuster, 1996), 206.

Chapter 14: The Light Shining

1. Frederick Buechner, *Telling the Truth: The Gospel As Tragedy, Comedy and Fairy Tale* (San Francisco: Harper & Row, 1977), 90.

2. Smedes, *Forgive & Forget*, 168.

3. Sittser, *A Grace Disguised*, 37-8.

4. Viktor Frankl, *Man's Search for Meaning* (New York: Simon & Schuster, 1963), 104.

5. Martin Luther King Jr., *Strength to Love* (Philadelphia: Fortress Press, 1963), 152.

6. Smedes, *Forgive & Forget*, 96.

7. King Jr., *Strength to Love*, 53.

8. C. S. Lewis, "On Three Ways of Writing to Children," as quoted in Walter Hooper, *Past Watchful Dragons* (New York: Collier Books, 1971), 1.

9. Special thanks to James Oliphint for bringing this scene from the movie to my attention and for the contribution it made to illustrate the blessing.

Chapter 15: To Get the Message

1. Robert Fulghum, *All I Really Need to Know I Learned in Kindergarten* (New York: Random House, 1986, 1988), 191.

2. Fulghum, *All I Really Need*, 191.

3. "Diana: Portraits of a Lady," *Life*, November 1997, 14.

4. Germaine Greer, "Unmasking the Mother," *Newsweek*, 22 September 1997, 33.

5. Michael Satchell, "Death Comes to a Living Saint," *US News & World Report*, 15 September 1997, 12.

6. Michael O'Mara, *Diana, Princess of Wales: A Tribute in Photographs* (New York: St. Martin's Press, 1997).

7. Katrine Aimes, "A Mother and Her Sons," *Newsweek*, Commemorative Issue: "Diana, A Celebration of Her Life," 3 November 1997, 52.

8. Aimes, "A Mother and Her Sons," 52.

9. Satchell, "Death Comes to a Living Saint," 12.

10. Tom Masland, "A Touch of Humanity," *Newsweek*, Commemorative Issue: "Diana, A Celebration of Her Life," 3 November 1997, 66.

11. Masland, "A Touch of Humanity," 68.

12. Masland, "A Touch of Humanity," 68.

13. Masland, "A Touch of Humanity," 68.

14. Joanna Hurley, *Mother Teresa: A Pictorial Biography* (Philadelphia: Running Press, Courage Books, 1997).

15. Malcolm Muggeridge, *Jesus: The Man Who Lives* (New York: Harper and Row, 1987), 73.

Part 3: The Pictures We Leave Behind

1. Information on Robert E. Lee in this chapter is from J. William Jones, "Personal Reminiscences, Anecdotes, and Letters of General Robert E. Lee," in Douglas S. Freeman, *Robert E. Lee*, vol. 4 (New York: Scribner's, 1948), 206.

Chapter 20: Even Our Enemies

1. Abraham Lincoln, First Inaugural Address, 4 March 1861, *A Treasury of the World's Great Speeches*, comp. and ed. Houston Peterson (New York: Grolier, 1965), 512.

2. Adapted from a sermon by Martin Luther King Jr. entitled, "Loving Your Enemies," King Jr., *Strength to Love*.

31 Days to Creating Better Pictures

Day 1: Edith Schaeffer, *What Is a Family?* 189-90, quoted in Gladys Hunt, *Honey for a Child's Heart* (Grand Rapids: Zondervan, 1978), 89-90.

Day 2: Mary Bahr, *The Memory Box* (Morton Grove, Ill.: Albert Whitman & Company, 1992).

Day 3: Bryan Peterson, *People in Focus: How to Photograph Anyone, Anywhere* (New York: Watson-Guptill Publications, 1993), 8.

Day 5: John Kotre, *White Gloves: How We Create Ourselves Through Memory* (New York: Norton, 1995), 101-2.

Day 7: Schaeffer, *What Is a Family?* 192, quoted in Gladys Hunt, *Honey for a Child's Heart*, 89-90.

Day 8: Linda and Richard Eyre, *Teaching Your Children Sensitivity* (New York: Simon & Schuster, 1995), 92.

Day 9: C. S. Lewis, *Letters to an American Lady* (Grand Rapids: William B. Eerdmans Publishing Co., 1967), 117.

Day 10: Heiferman and Kismaric, *Talking Pictures*, 84-5.

Day 11: Gerald Locklin, "Learning to See Crooked," *Children of a Lesser Demagogue* (Stockton, Calif.: Wormwood Review Press, 1988). Used by permission of the author.

Day 13: W. Livingston Larned in *The Best of Gordon Owen* (self-published, n. d.).

Day 15: Schaeffer, *What Is a Family?* 200-1.

Day 16: Schaeffer, *What Is a Family?* 196-7.

Day 17: Eyre, *Teaching Your Children Sensitivity*, 93. Heiferman and Kismaric, *Talking Pictures*, 93.

Day 19: Frederick Buechner, *The Wizard's Tide* (San Francisco: HarperSanFrancisco, 1990), 44-6. Reprinted by permission of HarperCollins Publishers, Inc.

Day 20: Bruno Bettelheim, "Exploring Childhood As an Adult," *Reclaiming the Inner Child*, ed. Jeremiah Abrams (Los Angeles: Jeremy P. Tarcher, 1990), 284.

Day 20: Hunt, *Honey for a Child's Heart*, 47.

Day 21: Marjorie Holmes, *Who Am I God?* (New York: Doubleday, 1970, 1971), 16.

Day 22: Hunt, *Honey for a Child's Heart*, 20-1.

Day 23: Adapted, Bruce Larson, *The One and Only You* (Waco, Texas: Word Books, 1974), 84-5.

Day 24: Kotre, *White Gloves*, 102-3.

Day 25: Heiferman and Kismaric, *Talking Pictures*, 88

Day 26: Adapted, Ashabranner, *Always to Remember*, 17.

Day 27: Heiferman and Kismaric, *Talking Pictures*, 9.

Day 28: Kotre, *White Gloves*, 100-1.

Day 29: Sittser, *A Grace Disguised*, 27-8.

Day 30: Norman Habel, *For Mature Eyes Only* (Philadelphia: Fortress Press, 1969), 28-9.

Day 31: Frederick Buechner, *The Sacred Journey* (San Francisco: Harper & Row, 1982), 6-7.

DATE DUE

HIGHSMITH #45230

Printed
In USA